Clinical Counsel
Medical Settings

Edited by Peter Thomas,
Susan Davison and
Christopher Rance

First published 2001 by Brunner-Routledge
27 Church Road, Hove, East Sussex, BN3 2FA

Simultaneously published in the USA and Canada
by Taylor & Francis Inc.
29 West 35th Street, New York, NY 10001

Brunner-Routledge is an imprint of the Taylor & Francis Group

© 2001 Peter Thomas, Susan Davison and Christopher Rance, selection
and editorial matter; individual chapters, the contributors.

Typeset in Times by Keystroke, Jacaranda Lodge, Wolverhampton
Printed and bound in Great Britain by T J International Ltd, Padstow, Cornwall

British Library Cataloguing in Publication Data
A catalogue record for this book is available from the British Library

Library of Congress Cataloging in Publication Data
Clinical counselling in medical settings / edited by Peter Thomas, Susan Davison, and
Christopher Rance.
    p. ; cm. — (Clinical counselling in context)
Includes bibliographical references and index.
ISBN 0–415–21717–2 (hbk) — ISBN 0–415–21718–0 (pbk)
    1. Counseling. 2. Psychotherapy. I. Thomas, Peter, 1957 July 29–
II. Davison, Susan, 1948– III. Rance, Christopher, 1938– IV. Series.
    [DNLM: 1. Counseling—methods. 2. Genetic Counseling methods.
3. Medical Staff—psychology. 4. Rehabilitation—methods. 5. Staff
Development—methods. WM 55 C64085 2001]
BF637.C6 C455 2001
616.8914—dc21   361.323   2001025162
                  THO

ISBN 0–415–21717–2 (hbk)
ISBN 0–415–21718–0 (pbk)

The editors would like to dedicate this volume to their parents, three of whom died during its preparation

Contents

Figures and appendices

Figures

Appendices

Contributors

Frances Birch is a psychodynamic counsellor in private practice. After qualifying in medicine at Cambridge she specialised in palliative medicine, becoming a consultant and hospice director. She has worked in general psychiatry at the Maudsley Hospital, London, where she is now an honorary clinical associate attached to the Psychotherapy Department.

Emma Coore BSC, MBBS, DROG is a general practitioner currently working in a central London practice. She developed her interest in counselling through co-ordinating the study of primary care counselling in south London while completing her general practice training at King's College and the Maudsley Hospitals in London

Alison Jesson RGN, BSC(HONS), MSC (Psychotherapy), has had over 27 years of working in the National Health Service. She originally qualified as a nurse and subsequently as a UKRC counsellor and a UKCP psychotherapist. She works part-time as a staff counsellor in a large London teaching hospital. She also runs her own private psychotherapy practice, teaches interpersonal and managerial skills to health service staff, and works for a national employee assistance programme (EAP).

Alison Lashwood works as a genetic counsellor within a clinical genetics team at Guy's Hospital in London. Her principal interests are pre-symptomatic testing for those at risk of Huntington's disease and prenatal diagnostic testing. More recently she has become affiliated to the Guy's and St Thomas Hospital Centre for re-implantation diagnosis.

Amanda Logan is a nurse counsellor in the renal unit at a leading London teaching hospital.

Simon Lovestone is senior lecturer in old age psychiatry and neuro-science at the Institute of Psychiatry, London University, and honorary consultant old age psychiatrist at the Maudsley Hospital, London.

Mando Meleagrou works in the psychotherapy consultation service for pregnant women at the Harris Birthright Research Centre for fetal medicine at King's College Hospital London.

Kate Pugh BMEDSCI, MBBS, MRCPSYCH is a consultant psychiatrist in psychotherapy, Gordon Hospital, London. She has experience in working with GP counsellors, running a Balint group for 5 years during senior registrar psychotherapy training at the Maudsley Hospital, and facilitating, with Dr Emma Coore, on outcome study of GP counselling. She is currently consulting to community mental health teams and GP practices in Pimlico, London.

Angela Taylor BA(HONS) has worked in the National Health Service as a rehabilitation counsellor for 6 years. She is currently the senior counsellor in rehabilitation medicine for a rehabilitation centre in south London. Much of her work has involved the theme of loss, particularly in healthcare.

Maureen Williams is a chartered clinical psychologist employed by the South London and Maudsley NHS Trust as a consultant psychologist to provide a clinical service to medical and surgical patients, both in- and out-patients at King's College Hospital London. For the past 18 years she has provided an assessment and treatment service to the King's pain relief unit. She has published research on pain patients, lectured at international conferences on the management of chronic pain patients and is honorary senior lecturer at the Institute of Psychiatry, University of London.

Editors

Susan Davison PHD, MBBS, MRCP, MRCPSYCH is a psychoanalyst and consultant psychotherapist to the South London and Maudsley Hospital NHS Trust.

Christopher Rance OSB (OBL PK), BSC, MBCS, MINST GA is a management consultant, group analyst, psychotherapist and lecturer in organisational group analysis at London and Hertfordshire Universities.

Peter Thomas MSC, RGN is a senior counsellor and counselling consultant in a number of healthcare organisations, including mental health, general practice and primary care groups.

Introduction

Susan Davison

In considering whom to invite to contribute to this book we became aware
of the many counsellors known to us personally who are working in a
wide variety of medical settings. It appears that an army of counsellors
has sprung up from the dragon's teeth of modern technological medicine.
The growth of this area of application of counselling has occurred without
any central policy planning; rather the case for it has been made on the
spot, by the professionals who identified the need for it.

Apart from genetic counselling, which is an exception, the story is
of Trojan horses in the form of researchers or members of staff who also
happen to have a training in psychotherapy and counselling. Almost
universally the idea of having a person whose role it is to listen to what
may not be spoken, to articulate what the client may be too frightened to
accept, to acknowledge beliefs and feelings unacceptable to the staff as
a whole, can be threatening. Why should this be? We have hypothesised
that in general those who are committed to the effective application of
sophisticated technology often find it difficult to accept that psychological
interventions can also be an important contribution to the welfare of
patients.

Our initial plan was to edit the contributions to this book in a way
which would provide a consistency of style and structure. However, it
became clear to us that the style of each contribution in itself reflected the
way in which the context influenced the attitudes and approaches of each
practitioner. We have therefore left the contributions in the style in which
they were originally provided as being in itself a comment on the influence
that context has on the mode of counselling.

Isabel Menzies Lyth is quoted again and again by our contributors,
indicating the centrality of the link between the organisation of a human
institution and the need of the staff to employ psychological defences in
order to be able to perform their professional duties without unmanageable

emotional cost. It may have been realistic to combine the functions of physical care and good counsel when in truth there was little to be done other than let nature take its course. But today even hospice care of the dying has become increasingly technical.

Inherent in the medical settings described in this book is a tendency to let a rift form between the physical technical care and the psychological care of patients. This is not to criticise staff who must defend themselves from being overwhelmed by the emotional significance of what they do. The temptation to relegate psychological care to some less important realm, which at a pinch can be dispensed with, must be resisted. Counselling has made a utilitarian case for its inclusion in the multidisciplinary team. Patients appreciate it, and it takes a burden of care off the shoulders of the other healthcare professionals. It can feed back usefully into the way services are structured and delivered and it can point out the need for the care of the staff themselves. In this way the counsellor may contribute to the quality of service provided.

The ideal to which the multidisciplinary team aspires is that of creative collaboration between differentiated roles. This requires mutual respect, an understanding of each other's strengths and weaknesses, and good communication. A good team is one in which everyone feels valued for the contribution he or she makes. Good morale is the cornerstone of excellence of delivery of medical care. However, there always will be times when, for whatever reason, staff begin to feel persecuted, unappreciated, underfunded and overworked. This is fertile ground in which rifts can develop between professions. The counsellor, who is not within any of the existing hierarchies, may be sanctioned by the team to alert everyone to dips in morale and to recommend reflection on its causes so as to arrive at remedial action. However, there may also be a tendency to shoot the messenger.

Counselling in healthcare settings has grown so fast that regulatory organisations, such as the British Association of Counsellors and Psychotherapists (BACP), are struggling to keep up. Codes of practice and ethics, which were originally defined in relation to private practice, need to be re-examined in the context of multidisciplinary working. There is now a sufficient body of experience, partly drawn from counsellors in primary care, but now available from other medical settings as described here, from which to establish codes of practice for counsellors working with multidisciplinary teams. Issues of confidentiality in relation both to the clients' families and to the team, for example, need to be clarified in terms of optimising care on the one hand and protecting against paternalism on the other.

There is at present no formal training for counsellors in specialised medical settings. This has not proved to be a major handicap when counsellors are drawn from the ranks of the existing multidisciplinary teams. Their knowledge base with regards to the technical medical side of the service will be more than adequate. They will already be sensitised to the issues most likely to arise in the client population that uses the service, particularly if they had identified the need for counselling in the first place.

As the profession develops this will no longer necessarily be the case; appropriate training will need to be offered. Some form of accreditation will be required as a means of quality control. Suitable qualified professionals will not happily accept a situation in which they are seen as middle-class 'do-gooders' who don't really need an income. They will want, and should have, a proper career structure with appropriate pay scales and the benefits enjoyed by other healthcare professionals in the National Health Service (NHS).

With this raised professional profile and the attendant costs to the NHS budget, counsellors will need to demonstrate their value to the service. Genetic counselling, the most firmly established application in a medical setting, has begun to establish a methodology for evaluating its effect. Counselling is most readily legitimised when patients, in order to make informed decisions and to be able to co-operate fully with their care, need to understand the scientific basis of the advice being offered to them by their doctors. Genetic counselling most obviously conforms to this paradigm: an understanding of Mendelian inheritance and statistical probability are the basic tools with which to understand the chances of giving birth to offspring affected by genetic disease. The effect of a counselling intervention at this fundamental educational level could quite easily be measured.

This however is only the beginning as there are many obstacles to the assimilation of facts which have emotional significance. To be able to help a client and his or her family imagine the emotional consequences for them of the various outcomes and decisions ahead requires more than the ability to communicate complex ideas simply. It requires an understanding of psychological defences, for none of us can bear too much reality; it requires tolerance and patience and an awareness of different cultural and religious beliefs; it needs respect for the private beliefs and hidden meanings we all attribute to the fundamental processes of life and death. So much of the emotional work has to do with grief; clients and their families need to mourn the future they took for granted in order to be able to make a healthy adaptation to the reality of the condition and its often unpleasant treatments.

An effective counselling intervention should be able to be recognised, in terms of increased acceptance of reality, improved co-operation with treatment, better understanding of the danger signals of opting out of care, a more positive outlook on the future, and greater flexibility in adapting to disability. Suitable instruments to measure all these benefits have yet to be devised but this is an obvious area for properly co-ordinated, collaborative research of the type that has led to the development of the Clinical Outcomes in Routine Evaluation (CORE) instrument. It should also be recognised there can be no definition of benefit which does not involve a value judgement of some kind, one from which individual clients may dissent. Thus measurement of outcome of a process, which is intended to enhance the freedom of choice in the context of each individual's beliefs and values, can only ever be an approximate science.

An important role for the BACP, which already has some of the structures in place, will be to provide appropriate professional support to counsellors in medical settings. It is in a position to take the lead in developing professional standards and codes of practice, co-ordinating research and audit initiatives, negotiating appropriate terms and conditions for counsellors in the NHS, and laying down guidelines for supervision and care of staff. Not least, it can promote the cause of psychological care of patients and their families to those who determine policy and funding – our political masters. If counselling is to emerge as a new and valued profession in the health service it needs a professionally run body to represent it. Counsellors need to shake off the perception of some that they are from a voluntary army nourished by altruism rather than by a conviction of the importance of professional psychological care in the effective delivery of medical services.

The editors have not, as a matter of principle, sought to categorise counselling approaches according to particular theoretical or technical orientations. Some authors declare a particular category, others use eclectic integrative models. Our point is that the contexts both draw counsellors of certain theoretical inclinations to them and then influence the development of a particular style in that context.

Some case vignettes have been provided to illustrate counselling in action. All these vignettes have been anonymised so that not even the subjects could recognise them. If anyone thinks they do, then our major changes have resulted in an accidental correlation with someone unknown to us.

Chapter 1

A review

Emma Coore and Kate Pugh

Introduction

The remarkable growth of counselling in both the NHS and the voluntary sector signals a change in our culture over the past 20 years. General practitioners and their patients value highly the services of their practice counsellor, even when no measurable symptom reduction occurs (Hemmings 1999). Many hospital departments and clinics now employ counsellors to work as part of the multidisciplinary team so as to be able to take a more holistic approach to patient care. In a service where greater efficiency is being squeezed out of all health workers, the counsellor can offer a precious commodity – time. Time to listen; time to attend to questions that 'I didn't want to bother the doctor with'; time protected from the demands of emergencies and routines alike; time to assess how much a patient has understood about his or her condition, the treatment and the implications of it for his or her future and family.

Counsellors are being enlisted in increasing numbers to meet a need, perceived by healthcare workers and patients alike, to attend to the psychosocial aspects of modern medicine while the technocrats apply their amazing skills to the patient's condition. The ensuing chapters in this book will describe how counselling has been integrated into a number of different services, showing how the context and its conditions shape the counsellor's work and in turn how the counsellor can bring a new dimension to the service.

It has been argued that counselling is an indulgence, fostering dependence in patients whose unpleasant but probably self-limiting mental states should be born with stoicism (Persaud 1993). But this is to misunderstand the complexity of the problems which beset our patients. This chapter aims to set out, in general terms, the case for employing counsellors in medical settings and to outline the nature of the work involved.

There is a large amount of psychological adjustment needed in relation to many serious and non-serious medical conditions. Inevitably the degree to which this is necessary will vary from patient to patient. It is impossible to determine to what extent the problems are directly due to the illness and how much they are related to the patient's underlying psychological state. Similarly, when counsellors are working with psychiatric services or in general practice, distress may stem from many aspects of a patient's life, all of which may be worthy of counselling therapy if the patient's overall welfare is the aim.

There have been a large number of studies to determine the prevalence of psychological disorder amongst medical patients and these suggest that, compared to the general population prevalence of 9 per cent (Goldberg and Huxley 1980), the prevalence in hospital populations is around 30 per cent. For example, eighteen months following hysterectomy, 28 per cent (Gath *et al.* 1982); adjustment to haemodialysis: 53 per cent depression, 30 per cent anxiety (Kaplan de Nour 1981); psychological morbidity following stoma surgery over 50 per cent (Thomas *et al.* 1984). A general medical ward can be expected to contain 23 per cent (Maguire *et al.* 1974) to 29 per cent (Moffic and Paykel 1975) of patients with psychiatric morbidity, generally depression.

Counsellors in healthcare settings are often assisting patients to cope with some of life's potentially most challenging moments. Life events may have occurred which have been shown to play a significant role in the predisposition towards and onset of depression. Loss in some form or other may have occurred or be imminent. This need not relate just to death but to loss of mobility, independence, fertility or just future hopes, to name but a few (Murray-Parkes, 1976; Daniluk 1997):

> It is vital to understand the emotional reactions which grip people in these personal crises can have a crushing power. For some, the anguish of the emotional reaction is harder to bear than the illness itself.
>
> (Nichols 1984)

These reactions are faced by staff on a daily basis whilst working in hospices, renal units, infertility clinics and with any form of chronic illness or where conditions are not amenable to treatment.

Counselling as information and education

Other general aspects of medical settings that influence the work of counsellors include the trend towards giving patients more and more information about what is happening to them and the choices available to them. Health professionals are not always as skilled at imparting this information as would be ideal. Counsellors have been employed to provide information, with the focus being on effective communication with the patient, helping them to reach decisions about investigations and treatment options. In this way they can act as advocates for the patients to guide them through the illness and help them voice their needs and concerns. This is particularly common in fields where the most critical decisions are being made, for example, prior to termination of pregnancy, in genetic disease testing or transplant surgery. This sort of help for patients has been shown to increase their knowledge and reduce their anxiety about procedures such as angioplasty for cardiac disease (Tooth *et al.* 1997) and in epilepsy treatment (Jain *et al.* 1993). The same applies to the relatives of patients, especially of child patients, who often have a lot of questions about treatments but little opportunity to express their fears. Caring for carers in all fields of healthcare is a neglected but important part of the task (Ward and Cavenagh 1997).

A similar sort of work is being undertaken in the area of patient education. Here again effective communication with patients, including appreciating their view point, is essential in enabling them to adjust psychologically to their illness and to feel motivated and able to participate fully in their treatment. Examples include the counselling role of nurse practitioners in diabetes and post-myocardial infarct care where patient co-operation is essential for a good outcome (David *et al.* 1997; Martin *et al.* 1997). One method described to do this is 'dialogue medicine' (Hellstrom *et al.* 1998). This whole field is a very specialist area into which counselling has expanded and, though it is obviously different from more generic forms of counselling, it represents a significant aspect of counselling in medical settings.

The contexts of counselling

There are many different settings in which counselling is taking place that are a part of wider healthcare services. Each of these has unique features that also influence the counselling process. Rehabilitation services work on adaptation to injury or disability and so counselling in that setting is focused on adaptation to change, self-empowerment and regaining control

(Cain 1995; Oliver 1995). Hospices, on the other hand, are concerned with symptom control at the end of life and so counselling there is involved with decisions about when to stop life-sustaining treatment. These choices are dependent on the patients' and their relatives' understanding and acceptance of the illness and its potential outcomes (Stanley 1995). Spiritual issues are bound to play a part in counselling in both of these settings, perhaps more than would be expected in other areas of counselling (McCarthy 1995a, 1995b).

Staff counselling, in contrast, has other pressures which affect the process. The client's needs are affected by the culture of the employing authority, including the pressures put on staff (Goss and Mearns 1997) and fears about job security (Cummins et al. 1995; Smith 1997).

Even the nature of the clients themselves can be affected in some fields. In centres for genetic disease many of the patients are asymptomatic but are waiting for test results that will affect any children they may have. Often relatives who are not directly involved may be having tests and may also need counselling (Du et al. 1998). The populations eligible for testing will also vary, depending on knowledge about genetic linkages with disease (Lalloo et al. 1998). Therefore there is the potential to create new 'patient' populations and with it psychological need as people discover that they may develop conditions of which they would not otherwise have become aware for some years (Wahlin et al. 1997).

Lastly, one huge variable of counselling within medical settings is exactly who should be performing the counselling and where. At present there is great variation, particularly in the former. Health professionals have traditionally carried out the role, though increasingly specialist nurses or nurse practitioners are being employed to extend this work (Hulskers and Neiderer-Frei 1997). However, the need for counselling in healthcare has grown out of a recognition that there is a neglect of the psychological needs of medical patients and that there are powerful forces which limit the ability of health professionals to meet those needs.

On the one hand, there are time constraints on most professionals due to the continuous demand for more patients to be seen and more procedures completed. This does not always allow for the depth of enquiry into any one patient's psychological state as might be desired. Also health professionals may lack the skills to deal with certain situations where more specialised knowledge and experience is needed, for example in HIV counselling (Worm et al. 1998) and addiction (Arborelius et al. 1995; O'Connor et al. 1997).

On the other hand, there is a need for health professionals to remain impersonal and to maintain a degree of emotional detachment in order to be able to carry out their duties. The illness itself demands psychological adjustment by the patient but the healthcare setting is rarely able to facilitate this process as health carers themselves are inevitably defended to some extent against the psychological impact of the illness on their patients. These defences are required to bear the burden of clinical responsibilities without becoming overwhelmed with anxiety, but the cost is the neglect of psychological care, unless this is planned for in the provision of counselling (Nichols 1984).

Isobel Menzies Lyth (1959, 1988), in her study of nurses' behaviour and relationships in a large teaching hospital, showed how the development of relationships with patients was blocked by giving nurses a few tasks to perform on many patients, with a ritualisation of care and with denial of feelings in the staff and depersonalisation of the patients in their care.

The capacity of health carers to remain emotionally attuned to their patients is enormously variable, but the nature of the need for medical and surgical intervention often requires the organisation to operate in such a way that feelings are denied, and the use of the defences of splitting and projection dominate (Jaques 1955). Counsellors in medical settings may, therefore, allow the health carers to continue to do their tasks that require this 'process of detachment' (Leif and Fox 1963) while providing the listening and response required by the patient.

Doctors and nurses do provide counselling in the form of giving information to patients and facilitating their decisions about ongoing medical care, but this can differ from the role of the counsellor, who will provide a skilled response to the distress of their patients that may at times seem to have little to do with the complaint that is brought to the doctor.

Cawley (1977) defined three levels of psychotherapy. Doctors and nurses provide level one therapy, which is the empathic and facilitating response in a caring professional relationship. Trained counsellors provide level two therapy, which draws on training in a variety of specific models of psychotherapy, for example, problem solving, cognitive/behavioural and psychodynamic. Counsellors have an important role in assessing the needs of patients who could benefit from level three therapy. This third level comprises specialist psychotherapy services delivered by psychotherapists in mental health centres, for example, an NHS psychotherapy outpatient department.

The location for counselling

Counselling relating to healthcare work is largely taking place within the hospitals and clinics which provide specialist services. However, where more general emotional problems are being encountered, alternative environments could be better. Counsellors frequently operate private practices, which are able to accept self-referrals and offer help in a context entirely separate from the healthcare setting. The advantage of this can be clearly seen in the situation of staff counselling, where employment issues may be more openly discussed outside the employer's premises (Tehrani 1994). This may also be the case where a patient feels there have been problems in his or her relationship with healthcare professionals. However, the disadvantages of this separation of functions probably outweigh the benefits.

There are several advantages to counselling occurring in the health-care environment. First, it facilitates communication between all the professionals involved with a patient. This is essential for good medical practice, particularly in sensitive areas such as HIV care (Gibb *et al.* 1997). It avoids any misunderstandings or potential for manipulation in the doctor–nurse–counsellor–patient interactions (Jones *et al.* 1994). Collaborative relationships here have enabled professionals to give a consistent message to patients, encouraging them to play an active role in their disease management (Hyland *et al.* 1995; Papadopoulos and Bor 1995). Such relationships also bring a closer awareness of other professionals' working practices and have allowed closer links to develop between services, for example in psychiatry. This makes it easier for counselling clients to be seen by a psychiatrist when necessary (Owen 1991) and more acceptable for psychiatric patients to receive counselling for certain aspects of their illness (Buchkremer *et al.* 1997), a treatment favoured in public opinion surveys (Jorm *et al.* 1997). It also allows for skills transfer between professionals and an improvement in the quality of referrals for counselling. There is currently a real lack of skills transfer between psychiatry and general practice (Aoun 1997). Counsellors are well placed to help GPs in this area. Counsellors employed in specialist medical settings need to understand the various investigations and treatments their clients are undergoing, topics typically not covered in their training (Einzig *et al.* 1995). Some training in general practice is available through universities, partly funded by the Counselling in Primary Care Trust.

In general, face-to-face contact between professionals working with the same patients promotes greater mutual respect and understanding which can only improve the service offered.

Another advantage of counselling occurring in healthcare settings is the role the counsellor can play within the multidisciplinary team. In some situations difficult emotions may arise out of the work that affects the team. For example, if a patient has died unexpectedly or even committed suicide the team members may be left with feelings of helplessness and hopelessness that could hinder their ability to cope with their work (Abeler *et al.* 1997). If the counsellor can work with the team to promote acknowledgement of these issues then they may be resolved far more easily and morale may be greatly improved.

Similarly, when problems do arise with individuals in a team, the counsellor can assist with examining the organisational processes or team dynamics that are contributing to those individuals' distress rather than allowing one person to be a scapegoat for what may be quite a dysfunctional system.

Working with groups in medical settings

Group work with staff and patients is probably under-represented in the literature. We are aware of a number of examples of this, such as with staff on an oncology ward and a special care baby unit (Cowmeadow 1995); groups for survivors of sexual abuse in various settings; group work in hospices to examine attitudes towards facing terminal illness (Langley and Payne 1997); and even community-based groups to discuss views about illnesses such as HIV that may be widely affecting a community (Campbell and Rader 1995). These, combined with self-help programmes such as those that are available for managing obsessive compulsive disorder (Holdsworth *et al.* 1996), provide cheaper and potentially more cost-effective methods of delivering counselling in medical settings.

The cost-effectiveness of counselling

The cost-effectiveness of individual counselling has been questioned because one-to-one therapy for a total of several hours, even such as occurs in brief interventions, is relatively expensive to healthcare providers. This, however, has to be offset against the potential cost of the patient's continuing distress. Obviously, in personal or quality of life terms, the therapy, if effective, could be invaluable. Also, in cases where the patient somatises his/her distress and presents with physical symptoms, the cost to health services may build up. The patient may repeatedly consult about symptoms, frequently requiring multiple, potentially unnecessary investigations while the underlying psychological cause remains unresolved and even unacknowledged. Timely counselling, even if not with the patient's full enthusiasm, may be invaluable in breaking a cycle of frustrating, costly and ineffectual interventions that satisfy neither staff nor patient (Hemmings 1999).

Assessing the cost-effectiveness of all healthcare services is of increasing importance in the NHS today. All fields are expected to audit their work to prove its effectiveness and justify ongoing funding. This includes counselling services, as is emphasised by Hiebert (1997). However, there is little agreement in the literature as to how best to evaluate counselling. Unless the effectiveness of services can be adequately proven, there is no way to assess cost-effectiveness. There is obviously a need for further studies to be carried out, but by exactly what methods remains debatable.

There are a number of different viewpoints on how best to evaluate counselling and psychological therapies in general. Some researchers have taken a very scientist approach, focusing on the medical model of illness. These studies are based on pathological and idealistic viewpoints and use the randomised controlled trial as the 'gold standard' of methodology (Haverkamp 1995; House 1996a). Instruments have been developed to measure change in counselling, and the CORE (Connell *et al.* 1997), a self-rating questionnaire, has shown encouraging results, as opposed to the HONOS (Health of the Nation Outcome Scale) which is considered to be poorly suited to measure change in patients without psychotic illness.

Although there is seen to be a need for rigorous application of the scientific method, more qualitative approaches with interpretative data have also been used (Rennie 1994; Van Hesteren 1995). These are based on the assumption that the processes involved in counselling cannot readily be fitted into a trial protocol and much of what is beneficial cannot be detected by standardised questionnaires. Alternatives tried include informal observations on the counselling process by both counsellor and patient (Flynn 1994; Hiebert 1994), encouraging reflection on what really occurred rather than what the counsellor hoped was occurring (Irving and Williams 1995). Similarly, analysis of the most helpful and most hindering moments of the sessions (Grafanaki and McLeod 1995), that is, those that created the most depth of feeling, is useful in determining the patients responses to the process (Cummings *et al.* 1995; Stalikas and Fitzpatrick 1995). Significant events for the patient, occurring outside the sessions, can also be included as can the patient's narrative of the overall process of the sessions (Cummings and Halberg 1995; Morgan 1995; Howe 1996). Good relationships with the patients are needed in order to acquire this sort of information (Grafanaki 1996) and an ethical viewpoint on the whole process is likely to become relevant.

So far there has been little acceptance of these sorts of research methods within medical settings and no agreement as to what does constitute acceptable evidence of efficacy and accountability (Hutchinson 1997). Further discussion of the constructs of counselling is needed for agreement to be reached on evaluation methods (Young 1997). Evaluation processes need to be agreed with stakeholders of the services as part of a willingness to collaborate and reflect on work openly. Though this is a difficult area, evaluation is an integral part of counselling and compromise is needed on all sides.

A review of evidence for the effectiveness of counselling has been conducted by Hemmings (1999). In this he distinguishes between the efficacy research of randomised controlled trials (RCTs) and the measure of effectiveness in the application to the clinical environment ('field trials'). That is, the difference between 'research' and 'audit'. He acknowledges that little use had been made to date of RCTs in efficacy evaluation partly because, unlike medical or surgical procedures which can be replicated, there are few repeatable factors in a counselling situation and therefore RCTs are a poor tool for evaluation. More importantly, just because efficacy may have been demonstrated once in controlled, artificial circumstances, there is no reason to suppose it will necessarily be replicated in the clinical setting. Effectiveness (audit) studies, however, indicate a very high level of satisfactory outcome in clinical practice, irrespective of whether RCTs have been attempted. This is in common with many other procedures provided by the NHS which have never been subjected to RCTs but are provided because common sense and audit indicate their effectiveness.

There are always those patients who seem not to improve after therapy or even get worse. In such cases the counselling may have uncovered more serious or widespread psychological disorder of which the patient was not previously aware. This may at first lead to an increase in distress, though with skilled handling it may been seen as clarifying the problems so that further therapy can be planned or take place. It will be in the client's long-term interest to confront his/her difficulties, although the timing of such interventions would depend on his/her capacities to cope. For example, if the patient is physically ill and facing an uncertain future it may be most helpful to limit consideration to the most immediate issues by using a brief psychotherapy model. Also, a realistic view of what issues are ever likely to be amenable to therapy in that patient also has to be taken so as not to give false hope that can never be realised. The counsellor's role as assessor of the wider psychological and mental health issues here is of enormous importance. He or she has a key role in deciding, with the patient's agreement, what issues to pursue at that time and what to refer for more specialist therapy then or in the future.

Professional issues in counselling in medical settings

There are advantages and disadvantages to working within medical settings for the counsellors themselves. There is the potential for more personal and professional support from health professional colleagues as well as more managerial and clerical back-up than might be available to a private practitioner. Unfortunately counsellors do not always receive it; there is little excuse for this, given the emphasis on multidisciplinary working in the NHS in recent years.

The patients using the counselling service may also view it differently if it is based in a medical setting. There may seem to be less stigma attached to seeing the counsellor, the service may be more accessible and patients may perceive the service to be more confidential as this is something they would generally expect from healthcare services. Perception of confidentiality is a particularly important issue in working with adolescents (Milne 1995).

There are, however, disadvantages for counsellors in healthcare settings. One major area is the danger of losing autonomy over the way in which the work is done. First, most counsellors are expected to stick to time-limited work (Dartington 1995) as healthcare providers are unwilling to fund the extensive courses of therapy traditionally associated with psychodynamic practice. A limit of twelve sessions is commonplace, during which significant progress is expected. It is no surprise, therefore, that client-focused, problem-solving approaches are common, using an eclectic mix of theoretical perspectives. Counsellors have been shown to get more satisfaction from longer-term work (Warner 1995), though clients were equally satisfied with short-term interventions (Warner 1996) or even just one-off assessments (Manthei 1995), especially if these occurred soon after referral (Hicks and Hickman 1994).

Another important issue for counsellors is the fear of having their case-load limited. There is concern that any national guidelines for counselling in medical settings could be too prescriptive about the sort of cases that are suitable for counselling. Obviously there must be some limit to what is an appropriate counselling referral, but cases need to be matched accurately to each counsellor's skills, personal style and areas of competence. This can be achieved through departmental protocols, providing they are reviewed and revised regularly with the agreement of all parties (Monach and Monroe 1995). Assessment of the counsellor's areas of expertise needs to take into account experience and non-theory-based learning as well as academic study (Williams and Irving 1995).

This whole issue of counsellor competence has been a source of criticism of the services, especially in primary care (Monach and Monroe 1995). Recognised standards are expected in all professions, not just healthcare (Bell 1996), and it is the lack of co-ordination of these that has caused the problem. The setting of standards is complicated by the diverse backgrounds of counsellors, including in general and psychiatric nursing, social work and psychology (Clark *et al.* 1997). Each of these fields contributes something to that counsellor's approach to patients as well as the model of therapy in which the counsellor is trained. This only serves to emphasise the need for some overall system of accreditation leading to a national qualification to meet the demand for professionalism amongst counsellors (Clarkson 1995), though this is welcomed by all practitioners (House 1996a, 1996b). An example of this has been the British Association of Counsellors' Code of Practice and Ethics, though this stops far short of a professional register and is by no means agreed upon by all counsellors (Syme 1995). There is the Faculty of Healthcare Counsellors and Psychotherapists, the British Association for Counselling and Psychotherapists (BACP), which has developed standards of employ-ment and training and has recently joined with other groups to form the Counsellors in Primary Care steering group to agree standards of basic training and further qualifications for GP counsellors. With the best possible structures in place a more cohesive profession could result, as has been achieved in career counselling via the policy workbook (Bezanson and Riddle 1995).

The Association of Counsellors and Psychotherapists in Primary Care has recently been formed and is in the process of providing a register of recognised practitioners for primary care. The Counsellors in Primary Care Trust further promotes the professionalisation of counselling in primary care.

Health services also have a responsibility within this. First, it is the responsibility of those employing counsellors to be certain that the counsellor is appropriately qualified and experienced for the post. Second, the employer should ensure that the counsellor is given adequate time for record-keeping/administration and more specifically for supervision and ongoing study (Monach and Monroe 1995). This privilege is afforded to most other health professionals and is funded, as would any other aspect of their professional and personal development whilst in that employment (Wilson 1994).

Career structure and a guaranteed pay scale are two other benefits that employees should expect but which are lacking in healthcare counselling. Again the lack of any unitary professional body contributes to this. As well as setting standards, such an organisation could be expected to promote the employment rights of its members and ensure national equality of working conditions. It could also facilitate the relationships with other services that interact with counselling, such as psychology (Milton 1995) and specialist psychotherapy. Local strategies could be agreed that could be built into a geographically equitable service (Radley *et al.* 1997) instead of the current situation of a plethora of services in some areas while other areas struggle to maintain even the bare minimum.

Until such a representative organisation is established and recognised it is understandable that many counsellors shy away from the rigours of professionalism, opting instead for the relative freedom of a self-employed status. However, this does not bring the profession any closer to finding constructive ways of working in the wider context of healthcare that is so rapidly expanding.

All of these issues reflect the value placed upon the counsellors' input to the multidisciplinary team by both healthcare professionals and the counsellors themselves. Autonomy without loss of rights to employment benefits is something afforded to respected team members. It is important that counsellors are given the freedom to make decisions with patients about aspects of their care and life, as enabling patients to do this is a part of the essence of their job and skill. Removing this control could upset the delicate balance between the counsellor working as part of the multidisciplinary team while maintaining enough distance to provide fresh insight when other members of staff are either too involved or unable to empathise with the patient's situation. There is a danger that counsellors are seen as people who are available to pick up the cases that others find demoralising or frustrating without offering them any say in the planned care of those patients. At worst they might be expected to persuade patients to accept treatments that they would not otherwise accept or counselling might become a sidelined therapy meted out to all comers irrespective of need. All disciplines have cases that are difficult to manage and it is best if care is given by the whole team in a co-ordinated and open manner rather than pushing a problem from one discipline to another.

Good teamwork can only be achieved with open communication and some relinquishing of autonomy by both counsellors and healthcare professionals alike in order to ensure balanced and mutually supportive service delivery. New opportunities exist for practising this, for example with the development of primary care groups in the community (Primary Healthcare Development 1998). These will remove the employer/ employee split that can inhibit effective communication (Small and Conlon 1988) and will facilitate the development of local counsellor groups that can support individuals in their work. An awareness of institutional dynamics at every level (Lanman 1994; McLeod 1994) is necessary to create the respected, equal relationships that are best for optimal, holistic patient care.

In conclusion, counselling in medical settings is as much about adaptation to the environment as it is about the relationship with the patient: 'very caring people who would go to the ends of the earth for the client, but who didn't understand the need to fit in with the NHS' (Fisher 1997) are not going to facilitate organisational change. The essence of counselling in the NHS, to quote Helen Fisher's study again, is 'all about boundaries and containment . . . containing the client's and the counsellor's issues . . . and having clearly defined contracts and boundaries with the organisation and the clients is absolutely essential'.

References

Abeler, M., Dia, M.L., Frohlich, J., Fuchs, G., Mahnopf, A. and Rohrig, A. (1997) 'The suicide conference: an instrument for support of involved teams after inpatient suicides', *Psychiatric* **24** (5): 231–4.

Aoun, S. (1997) 'General practitioners' needs and perceptions in rural mental healthcare', *Australian Journal of Rural Health* **5** (2): 80–6.

Arborelius, E. and Thakker, K.D. (1995) 'Why is it so difficult for general practitioners to discuss alcohol with patients?', *Family Practice* **12** (4): 419–22.

Aronoff, D.N., McCormick, N.B. Byers, E.S. and McGill, U. (1994) 'Training sex researchers: issues for supervisors and students', *Canadian Journal of Human Sexuality* **3** (1): 45–51.

Bagley, C., Bolitho, F. and Bertrand, L. (1996) 'Using human inquiry groups in counselling research', *British Journal of Guidance and Counselling* **24** (3): 347–55.

Bell, D. (1996) 'Developing occupational standards for the advice, guidance, counselling and psychotherapy sector', *British Journal of Guidance and Counselling* **24** (1): 9–17.

Bezanson, M.L. and Riddle, D.I. (1995) 'Quality career counselling services: a developmental tool for organisational accountability', *Canadian Journal of Counselling* **29** (1): 3–13.

Booth, H., Cushway, D. and Newnes, C. (1997) 'Evaluation of counselling in primary care: how can research be made more useful for practitioners?', *Counselling Psychology Quarterly* **10** (1): 51–68.

Buchkremer, G., Klingberg, S., Holle, R., Schulze, M.H. and Hornung, W.P. (1997) 'Psychoeducational psychotherapy for schizophrenic patients and their key relatives or caregivers: results of a two-year follow-up', *Acta Psychiatrica Scandinavica* **96** (6): 483–91.

Cain, M.E. (1995) 'Transition from school to community life: implications for rehabilitation counsellors', *Journal of Applied Rehabilitation Counselling* **26** (4): 34–7.

Campbell, I.D. and Rader, A.D. (1995) 'HIV counselling in developing countries: the link from individual to community counselling for support and change', *British Journal of Guidance and Counselling* **23** (1): 33–43.

Cawley, R.H. (1977) 'The teaching of psychotherapy', *Association of University Teachers of Psychiatry Newsletter*, Jan.: 19–36.

Clark, A., Hook, J. and Stein, K. (1997) 'Counsellors in primary care in Southampton: a questionnaire survey of their qualifications, working arrangements, and case mix', *British Journal of General Practice* **47** (423): 613–17.

Clarkson, P. (1995) 'Counselling psychology in Britain: the next decade', *Counselling Psychology Quarterly* **8** (3): 197–204.

Connell, J., Barker, M., Evans, C. *et al.* (1997) *Clinical Outcomes in Routine Evaluation: Guidelines for Use, version I*, London: Mental Health Foundation.

Cowmeadow, P. (1995) Personal communication.

Cummings, A.L. and Hallberg, E.T. (1995) 'Women's experiences of change processes during intensive counselling', *Canadian Journal of Counselling* **29** (2): 147–59.

Cummings, A.L., Barak, A. and Hallberg, E.T. (1995) 'Session helpfulness and session evaluation in short-term counselling', *Counselling Psychology Quarterly* **8** (4): 325–32.

Cummins, A.-M. and Hoggett, P. (1995) 'Counselling in the enterprise culture', *British Journal of Guidance and Counselling* **23** (3): 301–12.

Daniluk, J. (1997) 'Helping patients cope with infertility', *Journal of Clinical Obstetrics and Gynecology* **40** (3): 661–72.

Dartington, A. (1995) 'Very brief psychodynamic counselling with young people', *Psychodynamic Counselling* **1** (2): 253–68.

David, S., Abou-Amara, S., Colin, C., Perret-du-Cray, M.H. and Thivolet, C. (1997) 'Evaluation of the hospital management of insulin-dependent diabetics', *Presse Med.* **26** (35): 1666–70.

Du, J.S., Bason, L., Woffendin, H., Zackai, E. and Kenwrick, S. (1998) 'Somatic and germ line mosaicism and mutation origin for a mutation in the L1 gene in a family with X-linked hydrocephalus', *American Journal of Medical Genetics* **75** (2): 200–2.

Einzig, H., Curtis, J., Curtis, G. and Basharan, H. (1995) 'The training needs of counsellors in primary medical care', *Journal of Mental Health UK* **4** (2): 205–9.

Fisher, H. (1997) 'Plastering over the cracks? A study of employee counselling in the NHS', in M. Carroll and M. Walton (eds), *Handbook of Counselling in Organisations*, London: Sage.

Flynn, R.J. (1994) 'Evaluating the effectiveness of career counselling: recent evidence and recommended strategies', in special issue: 'Issues and solutions for evaluating career development programs and services', *Canadian Journal of Counselling* **28** (4): 270–80.

Friedli, K. and King, M. (1996) 'Counselling in general practice: a review', *Primary Care Psychiatry* **2** (4): 205–16.

Gath, D., Cooper, P. and Day, A. (1982) 'Hysterectomy and psychiatric disorder', *British Journal of Psychiatry* **140**: 335–50.

Gibb, D.M., Masters, J., Shingadia, D., Trickett, S. Klein, N., Duggan, C., Novelli, V. and Mercey, D. (1997) 'A family clinic: optimising care for HIV infected children and their families', *Archives of Disease in Childhood* **77** (6): 478–82.

Goldberg, D. and Huxley, P. (1980) *Mental Illness in the Community*, London: Tavistock Press.

Goss, S. and Mearns, D. (1997) 'Applied pluralism in the evaluation of employee counselling', *British Journal of Guidance and Counselling* **25** (3): 327–44.

Grafanaki, S. (1996) 'How research can change the researcher: the need for sensitivity, flexibility and ethical boundaries in conducting qualitative research in counselling/psychotherapy', *British Journal of Guidance and Counselling* **24** (3): 329–38.

Grafanaki, S. and McLeod, J. (1995) 'Client and counsellor narrative accounts of congruence during the most helpful and hindering events of an initial counselling session', *Counselling Psychology Quarterly* **8** (4): 311–24.

Haverkamp, B.E. (1995) 'Against scientism in psychological counselling and therapy: a response', *Canadian Journal of Counselling* **29** (4): 318–23.

Hellstrom, O., Lindqvist, P. and Mattsson, B. (1998) 'A phenomenological analysis of doctor–patient interaction: a case study', *Journal of Patient Education and Counselling* **33** (1): 83–9.

Hemmings, A. (1999) *A Systematic Review of the Effectiveness of Brief Psychological Therapies in Primary Healthcare*, Staines, Middx: Counselling in Primary Healthcare Trust.

Hicks, C. and Hickman, G. (1994) 'The impact of waiting-list times on client attendance for relationship counselling', *British Journal of Guidance Counselling* **22** (2): 175–82.

Hiebert, B. (1994) 'A framework for quality control, accountability, and evaluation: being clear about the legitimate outcomes of career counselling', in special issue: 'Issues and solutions for evaluating career development programs and services', *Canadian Journal of Counselling* **28** (4): 334–45.

Hiebert, B. (1997) 'Integrating evaluation into counselling practice: account-ability and evaluation intertwined', *Canadian Journal of Counselling* **31** (2): 112–26.

Holdsworth, N., Paxton, R., Seidel, S., Thomson, D. *et al.* (1996) 'Parallel evaluations of new guidance materials for anxiety and depression in primary care', *Journal of Mental Health UK* **5** (2): 195–207.

House, R. (1996a) 'Audit-mindedness in counselling: some underlying dynamics', *British Journal of Guidance and Counselling* **24** (2): 277–83.

House, R. (1996b) 'The professionalisation of counselling: a coherent case against?', *Counselling Psychology Quarterly* **9** (4): 343–58.

Howe, D. (1996) 'Client experiences of counselling and treatment interventions: a qualitative study of family views of family therapy', *British Journal of Guidance and Counselling* **24** (3): 367–75.

Hulskers, H. and Niederer-Frei, I. (1997) 'Nurse practitioners as counsellors', *Pflege* **10** (2): 80–5.

Hutchinson, N.L. (1997) 'Unbolting evaluation: putting it into the workings and into the research agenda for counselling', *Canadian Journal of Counselling* **31** (2): 127–31.

Hyland, M.E., Ley, A., Fisher, D.W. and Woodward, V. (1995) 'Measurement of psychological distress in asthma and asthma management programmes', *British Journal of Clinical Psychology* **34** (4): 601–11.

Irving, J.A. and Williams, D.I. (1995) 'Critical thinking and reflective practice in counselling', *British Journal of Guidance and Counselling* **23** (1): 107–14.

Jain, P., Patterson, V.H. and Morrow, J.I. (1993) 'What people with epilepsy want from a hospital clinic', *Seizure* **2** (1): 75–8.

Jaques, E. (1955) 'Social systems as a defence against persecutory and depressive anxiety', reprinted in M. Klein, P. Heimann and R.E. Money-Kyrle (eds), *New Directions in Psychoanalysis*, London: Tavistock Publications, 1971.

Jones, H., Murphy, A., Neaman, G., Tollemache, R. *et al.* (1994) 'Psychotherapy and counselling in a GP practice: making use of the setting', *British Journal of Psychotherapy* **10** (4): 543–51.

Jorm, A.F., Korten, A.E., Rodgers, B., Pollitt, P., Jacomb, P.A., Christensen, H. and Jiao, Z. (1997) 'Belief systems of the general public concerning the appropriate treatments for mental disorders', *Social Psychiatry and Psychiatric Epidemiology* **32** (8): 468–73.

Kaplan de Nour, A. (1981) 'Prediction to adjustment to haemodialysis', in N.B. Levy (ed.), *Psychonephrology I*, New York: Plenum, pp. 343–75.

Lalloo, F., Cochrane, S., Bulman, B., Varley, J., Elles, R., Howell, A. and Evans, D.G. (1998) 'An evaluation of common breast cancer gene mutations in a population of Ashkenazi Jews', *Journal of Medical Genetics* **35** (1): 10–12.

Langley, E.A. and Payne, S. (1997) 'Light-hearted death talk in a palliative day care context', *Journal of Advanced Nursing* **26** (6): 1091–7.

Lanman, M. (1994) 'Psychoanalytic psychotherapy and student counselling', *Psychoanalytical Psychotherapy* **8** (2): 129–40.

Leif, H.I. and Fox, R.C. (1963) 'Training for detached concern in medical students', in H.I. Lief (ed.), *The Psychological Basis of Medical Practice*, New York: Harper & Row.

McCarthy, H. (1995a) 'Understanding and reversing rehabilitation counselling's neglect of spirituality', in special double issue: 'Spirituality, disability, and rehabilitation', *Rehabilitation Education* **9** (2–3): 187–99.

McCarthy, H. (1995b) 'Integrating spirituality into rehabilitation in a technocratic society', in special double issue: 'Spirituality, disability, and rehabilitation', *Rehabilitation Education* **9** 2–3: 87–95.

McLeod, J. (1994) 'Issues in the organisation of counselling: learning from NMGC', *British Journal of Guidance and Counselling* **22** (2): 163–74.

Maguire, C.P., Julier, B.L., Hawton, K.E. and Bancroft, J.H.J. (1974) 'Psychiatric morbidity and referral on two general medical wards', *British Medical Journal* **1**: (902): 268–70.

Manthei, R.J. (1995) 'A follow-up study of clients who fail to begin counselling or terminate after one session', *International Journal for the Advancement of Counselling* **18** (2): 115–28.

Martin, C.C., Cordoba, G.R., Jane, J.C., Nebot, A.M., Galan, H.S., Aliaga, M., Pujol, Ribera, E. and Ballestin, M. (1997) 'Mid-term evaluation of a help program for smokers', *Medicina Clinica (Barc)* **29** (109) 19: 744–8.

Menzies-Lyth, I. (1959) 'A case study in the functioning of social systems as a defence against anxiety: a report on the nursing service of a general hospital', *Human Relations* **13**: 95–121.

Menzies-Lyth, I. (1988) 'A psychoanalytical perspective on social institutions', in E. Spillius (ed.), *Melanie Klein Today*, London: Routledge.

Milne, J. (1995) 'An analysis of the law of confidentiality with special reference to the counselling of minors', *Australian Psychologist* **30** (3) 169–74.

Milton, M. (1995) 'The development of counselling psychology in a clinical psychology service', *Counselling Psychology Quarterly* **8** (3): 243–7.

Moffic, H.S. and Paykel, E.S. (1975) 'Depression in medical in-patients', *British Journal of Psychiatry* **126**: 346–53.

Monach, J. and Monro, S. (1995) 'Counselling in general practice: issues and opportunities', *British Journal of Guidance and Counselling* **23** (3): 313–25.

Morgan, O.J. (1995) 'Recovery-sensitive counselling in the treatment of alcoholism', *Alcoholism Treatment Quarterly* **13** (4): 63–7.

Murphy, A. (1999) 'Setting standards for counsellors in primary care: a united approach', *Newsletter of Counsellors in Primary Care* no. 1.

Murray-Parkes, C. (1976) 'The psychological reactions to the loss of a limb', in J.C. Howell (ed.), *Modern Perspectives in the Psychiatric Aspects of Surgery*, London: Macmillan, pp. 515–32.

Nichols, K.A. (1984) *Psychological Care in Physical Illness*, London: Chapman & Hall.

O'Connor, P.G., Farren, C.K., Rounsaville, B.J. and O'Malley, S.S. (1997) 'A preliminary investigation of the management of alcohol dependence with naltrexone by primary care providers', *American Journal of Medicine* **103** (6): 477–82.

Oliver, J. (1995) 'Counselling disabled people: a counsellor's perspective', *Disability and Society* **10** (3): 261–79.

Owen, I. (1991) 'Assessment for counselling and the psychiatric services', *Counselling* **2** (2): 287–9.

Papadopoulos, L. and Bor, R. (1995) 'Counselling psychology in primary healthcare: a review', *Counselling Psychology Quarterly* **8** (4): 279–89.

Pedder, J. and Brown, D. (1979) *Introduction to Psychotherapy: An Outline of Psychodynamic Principles and Practice*, London: Tavistock-Routledge.

Persaud, R.D. (1993) 'The "career" of counselling: careering out of control?', *Journal of Mental Health UK* **2** (4): 283–5.

Primary Healthcare Development (1998) *Simple Guide to Primary Care Groups*, London: PHD.

Radley, A., Cramer, D. and Kennedy, M. (1997) 'Specialist counsellors in primary care: the experience and preferences of general practitioners', *Counselling Psychology Quarterly* **10** (2): 165–73.

Rennie, D.L. (1994) 'Human science and counselling psychology: closing the gap between research and practice', *Counselling Psychology Quarterly* **7** (3): 235–50.

Sibbald, B., Addington, H.J., Brenneman, D. *et al.* (1993) 'Counsellors in English and Welsh general practices: their nature and distribution', *British Medical Journal* **306**: 29–33.

Small, N. and Conlon, I. (1988) 'The creation of an inter-occupational relationship: the introduction of a counsellor into an NHS general practice', *British Journal of Social Work* **18** (2): 171–87.

Smith, E. (1997) 'Private selves and shared meanings: or forgive us our projections as we forgive those who project into us', *Psychodynamic Counselling* **3** (2): 117–31.

Stalikas, A. and Fitzpatrick, M. (1995) 'Client good moments: an intensive analysis of a single session', *Canadian Journal of Counselling* **29** (2): 160–75.

Stanley, J.M. (1995) 'Medical ethics: when to stop treatment', *Journal of Internal Medicine* **238** (6): 551–8.

Syme, G. (1995) 'Between a rock and a hard place: an introduction to ethical issues', *Psychodynamic Counselling* **1** (3): 403–19.

Tehrani, N. (1994) 'Business dimensions to organisational counselling', *Counselling Psychology Quarterly* **7** (3): 275–85.

Thomas, C., Madden, F. and Jehu, D. (1984) 'Psychological morbidity in the first three months following stoma surgery', *Journal of Psychosomatic Research* **28**: 251–7.

Tooth, L., McKenna, K., Maas, F. and McEniery, P. (1997) 'The effects of pre-coronary angioplasty education and counselling on patients and their spouses: a preliminary report', *Journal of Patient Education and Counselling* **32** (3): 185–96.

Van Hesteren, F. (1995) 'Toward restoring some "punch" in counselling and therapy research and practice: a response to Martin', *Canadian Journal of Counselling* **29** (4): 324–8.

Wahlin, T.B., Lundlin, A., Bachman, L., Almqvist, E., Haegermark, A., Winblad, B. and Anvret, M. (1997) 'Reactions to predictive testing in Huntington's disease: case reports of coping with a new genetic status', *American Journal of Medical Genetics* **17** (3): 356–65.

Ward, H. and Cavanagh, J. (1997) 'A descriptive study of the self-perceived needs of carers for dependants with a range of long-term problems', *Journal of Public Health Medicine* **19** (3): 281–6.

Warner, R.E. (1995) 'Counsellor bias against shorter term counselling? A comparison of counsellor and client satisfaction in a Canadian setting', *International Journal for the Advancement of Counselling* **18** (3): 153–62.

Warner, R.E. (1996) 'Comparison of client and counsellor satisfaction with treatment duration', *Journal of College Student Psychotherapy* **10** (3): 73–88.

Williams, D.I. and Irving, J.A. (1995) 'Theory in counselling: using content knowledge', *Counselling Psychology Quarterly* **8** (4): 279–89.

Wilson, J.E. (1994) 'Is there a difference between professional and personal development for a practising psychologist?', *Educational and Child Psychology* **11** (3): 70–9.

Worm, A.M., Smith, E., Sorensen, H. and Haxholdt, H. (1998) 'Contact tracing as a part of HIV prevention: current practice and attitudes of general practitioners and hospital physicians; preliminary results', *Ugeskrift for Laeger* **160** (8): 1174–8.

Young, R.A. (1997) 'Evaluation and counselling: a reply to Hiebert', *Canadian Journal of Counselling* **31** (2): 138–40.

Chapter 2

Genetic counselling

Simon Lovestone and Alison Lashwood

Introduction

Counselling in the genetic context is, at present, a specialised activity carried out, for the most part, as part of dedicated genetic services. In the UK at least, this means that most genetic counselling is conducted by regional genetics departments – truly a super-specialised or tertiary service – and in most cases is provided for families with a clear risk of inheriting a monogenic disorder. However, as molecular medicine continues its seemingly relentless advance and as the genetic underpinning of disease, and beyond, deepens, it seems that genetic counselling must spread beyond the confines of specialised departments. Just how far this spread should be, whether to secondary or primary care or direct to consumers via public health initiatives or through commercial enterprises, is an increasingly pressing concern.

The work of genetic departments has been concerned, until very recently, primarily with disorders of childhood or infancy and with counselling for pregnancy-related issues. Increasingly the client group has expanded and inevitably the disorders of concern to a genetics department have been of ever-later onset. As the genetic basis of common diseases becomes understood the scope of genetic medicine widens and the context of genetic counselling broadens. It is increasingly likely that the genes responsible for varying individual risk of conditions such as heart disease, psychiatric disorders and diabetes will be identified, raising the question as to whether genetic counselling has a role to play in the management of affected individuals and their families.

What is genetic counselling?

Although often considered together, genetic counselling is not synonymous with genetic testing. The two processes are separable, with the consequence that some individuals receive considerable counselling even in the absence of available testing, but also include at least the possibility that the converse might occur – genetic testing without counselling. Importantly, when considering these two elements in the context of a resource-limited health service, the costs of genetic testing are lower than counselling, in many instances considerably so. Usually the provision of genetic counselling has preceded the ability to do genetic testing. However, as DNA testing for newly identified disease-genes becomes ever more rapidly available, rifts in the marriage between counselling and testing can appear.

If genetic counselling is not testing then what is it? A much quoted definition of genetic counselling is that it is a process:

to help the individual or the family to:

1 comprehend the medical facts, including the diagnosis, the probable course of the disorder and the available management,
2 appreciate the way heredity contributes to the disorder and the risk of recurrence in specified relatives,
3 understand the options for dealing with the recurrence,
4 choose the course of action which seems appropriate to them in view of their risk and their family goals and act in accordance with that decision,
5 make the best possible adjustment to the disorder in an affected family member and/or to the risk of recurrence in that disorder.

(Fraser 1974)

Genetic counselling meeting this description may be given by many different disciplines – clinical geneticists, secondary or primary care doctors, or specialist genetic nurse counsellors. Relatively little is known about whether these groups differ in their practice of counselling, or what makes a successful counsellor. As discussed below, however, outcome studies have begun to show that something works; considerably more process research is needed to know which are the important elements that contribute towards success in genetic counselling.

The context of genetic counselling

There are currently twenty-five specialist regional genetic centres in the UK accepting referrals from primary and secondary care. As these consultations are addressing issues of heredity they may involve discussion with individuals within a family or commonly with multiple family members. This can create complexities for the delivery of genetic counselling as it is likely that individuals within a family will have different needs and agendas, potentially leading to a conflict of interests. As a result further separate appointments are often necessary to target the needs of different family members.

Due to the complex nature of many genetic disorders and the need for a medical multidisciplinary approach, many of the centres organise joint genetic clinics with other medical specialities. Specialist genetic counselling is delivered by medically qualified clinicians and genetic counsellors who may have a professional nursing background or a scientific background with specific training in genetic counselling.

In some centres patients are offered a pre-clinic visit, usually by a genetic counsellor. Such visits help by gathering essential basic family information, establish what the patient expects from the genetic consultation, and assess whether there are any particular psychological or social issues to be addressed in connection with the genetic risk or diagnosis.

Genetic counselling referrals fall broadly into a number of categories, including individuals or couples who have had a child or fetus affected with an inherited disorder, adults affected by or at risk of an inherited disorder and couples who are at increased risk of recessively inherited disorders because of consanguinity or ethnicity. For many individuals seeking genetic counselling the issues can be dealt with in one appointment; however, for others the nature of the referral or the decisions that need to be made with regard to genetic testing or prenatal testing dictate that a series of appointments will be required.

The diagnosis of a genetic condition and its mode of inheritance by its nature often shifts the focus of issues relating to an individual or couple to the extended family, and in doing so may raise anxiety amongst relatives and highlight the responsibility of the individual first identified as carrying the faulty gene for dissemination of this information.

The referral of a pregnant woman and her partner for genetic counselling for the first time often represents a complex and difficult situation for the genetic counselling professional. The gestation period of a pregnancy imposes a condensed time constraint on the counselling process. This will mean coming to terms with a diagnosis, making decisions about prenatal testing and consideration of termination of pregnancy within a time frame that is dictated by limitations of the availability of prenatal testing and the moral acceptability of second or third trimester termination. Under such circumstances the process of genetic counselling would attempt to provide the information necessary for the parents to make an informed decision and to support them at this stage. It affords the opportunity for continuing contact with the couple and future follow-up after the outcome of the pregnancy, whether termination or the birth of an affected child.

Case I

MN and OP were referred for genetic counselling by a midwife in a local antenatal clinic. MN was 19 years old and 12 weeks into her first pregnancy. Her 27-year-old husband OP was her first cousin, related through their fathers. The pregnancy had been planned and no problems had been reported, but the midwife had raised the issue of their consanguinity with them and they had asked for a genetics referral.

At their first appointment the issue of the risk of a recessive disorder in the pregnancy was explained and the couple seemed relieved that the 3 per cent risk figure was not higher. Discussions moved on to what could actually be offered in the form of screening. As the couple were both of Caucasian descent the option of screening for cystic fibrosis (CF) carrier status was discussed. At this stage the possible outcomes of this screening test were highlighted, including questions about how they would cope if they were both found to be carriers. The possibility of prenatal diagnosis, if this were the outcome, and the chance of having an affected child were discussed. One concern at this point was that they appeared to want reassurance and felt that the chance of the converse situation applying was small.

One week later the result of the CF carrier screening indicated that they were both carriers and the chance of their pregnancy being affected was increased to 1 in 4. MN and OP were seen again and although surprised by this news they did not appear to be too concerned. Prenatal diagnosis was discussed, as was the possibility of a referral to a paediatrician to discuss the implications of having a child with CF. Unhesitatingly they opted for prenatal diagnosis at 14 weeks' gestation after discussion about what could be offered if the pregnancy were affected. The implications of termination at this stage of pregnancy were focused upon.

One week later the results indicated that the pregnancy was affected with CF. The couple had spent much of the waiting time discussing their options with family and friends and MN had spontaneously contacted a relevant support group and spoken with the parent of a child with CF. She indicated that she was certain that she could not cope with a disabled child and her husband concurred. Two days later MN underwent termination of pregnancy.

Contact by letter was made shortly after the termination but the offer of an appointment was declined. Six months later MN rang to arrange an appointment, but cancelled at short notice; no reason was given. At about 12 months after their first consultation MN rang in a distressed state to request another consultation, indicating that she felt she was not coping and deeply regretted the termination of pregnancy.

The genetic counselling process at this stage had shifted into 'make the best possible adjustment to the disorder in an affected family member and/or to the risk of recurrence in that disorder'. MN attended the clinic with OP and they quickly explained that they were now living apart. MN had asked for 'some space' and described how frightened she was of contact with OP as this reminded her of the termination and she felt fearful that contact with him would lead to another pregnancy. She felt that gradually over the months she was not 'moving on' after the loss of her baby and now, as the anniversary of the termination loomed, she was unable to see any future for their relationship. It was also apparent that there was external pressure from other family members to make the marriage work, and the family dynamics were complicated by the fact that OP was living with MN's parents. MN described symptoms of insomnia, nightmares, agoraphobia, eating disturbance. She had recently given up her banking job as she felt unable to cope with organising her life on a daily basis. At this stage, following further discussion, she was eager to be referred on to a psychiatrist allied to the genetic counselling team for assessment.

This case illustrates how the process of genetic counselling works in practice and how patients are managed in less than ideal circumstances. This couple may well present again in the future if their situation changes and they consider another pregnancy.

The process of genetic counselling

Genetic counselling aims both to give information and to help individuals to come to terms with and use the information. In this respect it is different from many other forms of counselling. In other aspects, especially in the emphasis given to a non-directive process, genetic counselling has much in common with other forms of counselling. However, it is questionable whether either the overt aims or claimed processes of genetic counselling match what actually occurs in the counselling process. First, although the agenda of the counsellor may be to discuss the disease and its inheritance, the client may have other more pressing concerns. Evidence suggests that in many cases counsellor and client agree that what is needed is genetic information but that for a significant number of clients or in a significant part of many counselling sessions, there are needs for psychological support. Although the context is genetic, the issues causing distress may be wider.

Genetic counselling then may not always be about genetics; equally the process of genetic counselling may not always be as non-directive as claimed. Whilst almost all genetic counsellors claim to use non-directive counselling, only a third of secondary care specialists do so (Marteau *et al.* 1994). It may be difficult not to do so, particularly when the nature of the information handled during the session is so frequently ambiguous, and yet clients require clear-cut information in order to make clear-cut decisions (van Zuuren *et al.* 1997). For some decisions non-directiveness may not only be difficult to achieve but may actually be misplaced.

Does genetic counselling work?

Outcome studies in genetic counselling, as in all other forms of psychotherapy, have proven easier to conduct than process studies and a considerable body of evidence has accumulated to suggest that counselling is efficacious. Outcome has been assessed in terms of satisfaction, knowledge and psychological distress. Not surprisingly, genetic counselling programmes report a high level of consumer satisfaction, although whether this translates to improved health or well-being of those counselled is not known. Knowledge of the condition and risk has been shown to improve after counselling and this has been used as a surrogate marker for efficacy; although again, whether improved knowledge can be equated with improved health or well-being is at least open to question. Michie *et al.* (1997), for example, demonstrated that following counselling the level of knowledge was high but was not correlated with either satisfaction or psychological distress. Knowing may not be enough. Finally, genetic counselling decreases psychological distress – variously measured as anxiety or symptoms on scales such as the General Health Questionnaire. Following genetic counselling for breast cancer, for example, distress decreased even in those individuals who were given an increased personal risk estimate (Cull *et al.* 1999). These data all point to some, perhaps limited, efficacy of genetic counselling – worry and distress are decreased but not abolished; knowledge and understanding are increased but not completely.

Genetic counselling in Huntington's disease

Huntington's disease (HD) is a disorder most often affecting people in the fifth decade of life but occurring at all ages from childhood to old age. An uncommon disorder, it results in death over a period of a decade or more of neuro-degeneration affecting invariably the motor system but also causing psychiatric symptoms of depression and psychosis and, in the late stages, dementia. With the discovery of the gene for HD in 1993, direct genetic testing based only upon the DNA from an unaffected individual became possible. The test itself is very accurate and the result available to the individual absolute in almost every case. Inheriting the mutation results in disease. There are no known exceptions.

Who would want to know this sort of information? Before the direct test was available, a majority of individuals from affected families indicated that they would 'want to know' if they carried the gene. However, only relatively few eligible individuals proceeded with indirect testing by linkage. For some individuals the ambivalent nature of the information obtained by indirect testing (high vs. low risk) and the need to involve family members may have been sufficient to put them off having the test; for others the process of counselling may have played a part in the final decision. Of those who do decide to proceed with the test, follow-up studies have demonstrated an improved overall psychological state up to a year after testing (Wiggins *et al.* 1992), but a proportion of even those receiving a 'good news' result have some evidence of increasing stress or anxiety (Lawson *et al.* 1996).

Our experience with individual patients suggests that this does in fact occur and for some may be due to survivor guilt – with relatives being affected. For others the good news that they are not going to develop HD brings into relief the fact that they had been living their lives 'on hold' in the knowledge that they were at risk. All those life decisions not acted upon or carried through become cause for regret.

The protocols established by consensus groups for HD suggest that during counselling at least two sessions separated by three months should be given (Simpson *et al.* 1993). Two counsellors work together, the same counsellors being present on each occasion. It was agreed by consensus that testing of minors should not be performed, although interestingly those working with the young people question this view. Prenatal testing also carries difficult moral and personal decisions. In the worst case a counselled woman might present pregnant and ask for prenatal testing. Clearly the three month 'cooling off' period is not in this case possible, and a woman could learn within a very short space of time that she carries the gene and so too does her fetus. Although strenuous efforts are made to prevent these worse-case scenarios, it is not always possible. Finally, testing those suffering form psychiatric illness – either significant depression or psychosis – is problematical for obvious reasons.

The aim of counselling in predictive testing for HD, as for other disorders, is to ensure that the counselled person has adequate information about the disease and its inheritance to make a decision that they will not regret.

Case 2

AB, a 20-year-old man, was accompanied to the clinic by a friend and his friend's mother. A family history was taken, although at times AB was reluctant to discuss this, stating quite clearly that he didn't think it was relevant to the counselling session. His father was affected by HD when AB was an infant; his mother had frequent episodes of depression. AB recalled a disturbed early life with much of it spent in the care of his grandparents. When he was 10 his father died and soon after AB was placed in care as his mother experienced one of many repeated episodes of mental illness. He remained in care for most of the rest of his childhood.

After leaving social services' care AB had attended college but never completed a course and had drifted in and out of a number of unskilled jobs. He had few friends other than the one accompanying him to the counselling appointment. He had met her while working for her father and had subsequently become a friend of the family, living with them for a short while; but even after he rented his own flat he joined them regularly for meals.

During the first counselling session AB appeared defensive and some-what confrontative, being reluctant to engage in discussion but simply wanting to proceed to testing. He failed to see the purpose or necessity of counselling and felt it was just another attempt by the authorities to prevent him from getting what he wanted. He seemed somewhat surprised, perhaps disarmed, when from the outset both counsellors readily adopted the position that testing was available for him. His thoughts underlying the decision to have predictive testing were explored, first by open questioning and then by direct questioning, suggesting some of the many reasons given by others undergoing testing. There were no plans to have children and indeed he was not in a steady relationship. He did not believe he would change his life in any way as a result of the test. There were no issues relating to employment or insurance. It seemed he simply wanted to know whether or not he carried the mutation.

Some at-risk individuals become, unsurprisingly, preoccupied with the possibility of acquiring HD, and every stumble, every memory lapse raises fears that the disease is starting. This did not appear to be the case for AB: he thought very little about HD, was concerned but not pre-occupied, and on assessment of his mental state showed no evidence of depression or anxiety. During the session he did not appear to be interested in learning more about HD, although notably, both his friend and his friend's parent were, and it turned out that both had encouraged him to attend meetings of the HD association and had attended one meeting themselves.

This first session left both counsellors feeling somewhat dissatisfied – as though there were other issues that had not been discussed. AB agreed that he would consider carefully his motivation for seeking testing and the impact that this would have on his life. He left seeking a guarantee that he would be tested on his next visit. After discussion following this session the counsellors noted that AB had little control in his life and that this was largely, although not entirely, attributable to HD. Partly because of his father's illness, he had had periods in care and an unstable childhood. One possibility occurring to the counsellors was that he felt defined by HD and that having the test was one response to this – a way of taking control in order to diminish it. Taking control seemed important to him at this point in his life and it was felt his somewhat confrontative attitude was a learnt response to authority, again in order to demonstrate that he was able to take responsibility for himself.

With this formulation in mind he was seen again after the routine three-month wait. On this occasion the counsellors started the session by assuring him that the decision to take the test was his and his alone and that he could have the test that day. Since the previous session he had thought relatively little about the test, although he was keen to emphasise that he still wanted to proceed. The counsellors introduced the idea of testing at different times: some people decide to have a test before having children; others in order to determine their own children's *a priori* risk; others before important decisions such as whether to change job or to move house. AB's plans for the future were explored and he was invited to consider what impact knowledge of carrying the mutation might do to any developing relationship. Following this discussion it was agreed between AB and the counsellors that he would have the test but at some point in the future. He was offered another appointment but declined, saying he would contact the department when the time was right.

These sessions with AB illustrate that the outcome of genetic counselling may be the decision not to test and is an attempt to illustrate an example of the need in genetic counselling to be aware of possible psychological issues – to go beyond the gene when exploring the decision to be tested. Other powerful examples have been given by those receiving counselling themselves (Marteau and Richards 1996).

Genetic counselling in Alzheimer's disease

Although HD is a rare monogenic disorder, many of the lessons learnt during the past decade of counselling in HD genetics can be applied to genetic counselling for cancer and for Alzheimer's disease. AD can occur as a single gene disorder – early onset, autosomal dominant and very rare (reviewed in Hardy 1996). For these families genetic counselling and, in many cases, genetic testing, can be provided, the issues and protocols being identical to those for HD. The real challenge for the development of genetic counselling is late onset AD. Family history is one of the strongest risk factors for AD (Slooter and van Duijn, 1997) and careful pedigree studies have demonstrated a cumulative incidence in first-degree relatives rising to 50 per cent or more by the age of 90 years. Experience of working with families suggests that some have been concerned about inheriting Alzheimer's disease. In line with this, the most frequently raised subject on a helpline for those concerned about dementia was that of genetics (Harvey *et al.* 1998). One gene that increases risk of late onset AD has been unequivocally identified: the apolipoprotein E (APOE) gene (reviewed in Growdon 1998). Other genes have been putatively associated with AD and, when reported, a number of these discoveries have received considerable press attention. Variation in the APOE gene alters the risk of suffering from AD but does not cause it in the same way that mutations in the HD gene cause HD. Various consensus groups have considered the use of APOE testing and all are agreed that the data available on the relationship between the gene and the disorder are insufficient to recommend testing for susceptibility at the present time (Lovestone and Harper 1994).

Although genetic testing for late onset AD has little perceived utility, at least in the UK at present, this is a rapidly developing field. Genetic advances in AD receive wide publicity and it is possible that genetic testing will find some limited use in the foreseeable future either to enhance diagnosis or to aid clinical management. The questions are: Should genetic testing for this late onset condition proceed, even in affected patients, without counselling? If there is to be counselling, then who should do it and how? The answers to these questions might have wide relevance for the future development of clinical genetics.

A genetic counselling clinic for late onset Alzheimer's disease

As a first step to answering these questions and because of concerns that relatives of patients with Alzheimer's disease are often not able to access reliable and up-to-date information, we established a dementia genetics clinic at the Maudsley Hospital to meet some of these concerns. The aims were to offer information to relatives and to provide a preliminary assessment prior to genetic counselling for those for whom it was appropriate. We have adopted a model of a predominantly tertiary referral clinic run in collaboration with the Regional Genetics Service based at Guy's Hospital.

We expected to be providing a service to members of multiply affected families with predominant early onset. However, on average only one or two individuals per family have been affected and the age of onset of the youngest affected family member was 80 years of age. Those seen in the clinic, then, are little different from the relatives of all AD patients: they represent neither particularly familial nor particularly young pedigrees. Despite this, many of those seen in the clinic have themselves been assessed for memory loss, a number have been investigated and many had seen a number of different specialists. Clearly this is a group of highly concerned individuals whose needs are not being met by current services. More than half of those seen were either very anxious or clinically depressed, were receiving treatment from a specialist or were referred after having been seen in a clinic.

Case 3

EF is a lady within the age range of risk for late onset AD. She had witnessed the start of late onset dementia in all four of her siblings and a maternal uncle and maternal grandfather were also affected by late onset dementia. Her mother died in late age entirely free from dementia. She was very concerned about her own memory and the risk of suffering from Alzheimer's disease, which she estimated at far greater than 50 per cent. Nearly every day she found herself thinking about AD and every time she could not place someone or went into a room forgetting why she had done so she became convinced that this was the start of AD. Her knowledge of AD was extensive and she knew about mutations in the three genes causing autosomal dominant AD. She reasoned that with so many affected then this must be autosomal dominant AD and that she was at high risk. Her estimate of being at greater than 50 per cent risk was because all of her siblings were affected. She had taken a number of actions based upon this risk estimate including making a will and establishing an enduring power of attorney.

On discussing her concerns it became clear that, although she was worried for herself, she was most concerned for her children and grandchildren. She felt guilty because she was convinced she had passed on the gene and had read that autosomal dominant AD had an early onset; therefore her children would be struck down early in life and her grandchildren still earlier. Just recounting these fears made her tearful and anxious. However, these fears were groundless. Although she had many relatives affected, all were entirely free from disease until they had reached advanced years. The two more distant affected family members were separated from her siblings by her mother, who lived well into the age of risk without suffering from dementia. Given this, she was reassured that autosomal dominant AD was highly unlikely and that, although her children may be at some increased risk, they would not be at any greater risk than the general population of developing early onset AD. The difference between genetic factors causing AD and increasing risk of AD was explained and she was given an information sheet produced for Alzheimer Disease International explaining the various genes associated with AD.

Case 4

GH was referred by the specialist caring for her mother, who had AD, because GH was concerned about inheriting AD. In addition to her mother, an aunt was also affected by AD and was in a nursing home. There was no other family history. GH had no knowledge of AD genetics but was aware that there were genes involved as she had read about this in her newspaper. She had become preoccupied with inheriting AD and attributed every minor memory lapse to the disease and had pending a referral to a neurologist for investigation. During the counselling session she was given further information regarding AD genetics and the difference between genes causing autosomal dominant early onset AD and genes that increase risk of late onset AD. Like many people attending the clinic, she appeared to find reassuring the information that with a first-degree relative affected her risk was indeed increased but that this increase would not be manifested until she was herself over the age 70–80. Much of the session, however, was devoted to discussing her fears for her mother's future and the nature of AD. She had not understood the nature or purpose of the medication her mother was receiving nor the likely prognosis or treatment plans. It was agreed both that she would contact the Alzheimer's disease society for further information and would seek an appointment with her mother's care-team to discuss her management further. A letter describing the content and outcome of the session was sent to her and, with her permission, to the consultant caring for her mother.

Conclusions

The work of the AD clinic differs markedly from conventional genetic counselling in that the index disorder is one of old age, is common and is associated with genes that increase risk but do not cause the disorder. The counselling in this context is certainly divorced from genetic testing and yet the content has some similarities to that of the HD clinic described above. Our impression is that those attending the clinic are in need of factual information and the space to discuss their fears. Almost all had been told at some point not to worry because late onset AD was not inherited to a significant degree. This information, given with the best intentions and meant to reassure, did not in most cases match their own experience (their own family) or the information they received in the popular media. It is, in truth, also not correct. Late onset AD does have a genetic component and having a relative affected does increase risk but this risk is only manifested late in life. However, those attending the clinic have concerns not limited to themselves and to AD. A considerable number have worries and anxieties elsewhere in their lives and a number have had frank depression. In these cases help elsewhere was sought. Many of those attending the clinic were in need of information and support regarding their relatives affected by AD. Perhaps this should be available elsewhere; perhaps it was, but somehow these individuals' needs were not met.

Future work will determine whether the counselling in this clinic has any effect on these concerns and worries. The premise of this Alzheimer's disease genetics clinic is that information is empowering, although whether this has a lasting effect on reducing anxiety is not known. However, as our understanding of the genetics of Alzheimer's disease advances, clinicians will have to respond and this model of a collaboration between old-age psychiatry and a department of clinical genetics is one possible way forward. As other conditions from cancers to cardiac disease reveal their genetic component, then genetic counselling might become an increasing part of the medical mainstream.

Summary

This chapter presents a counselling process which is intimately linked to a medical routine, namely genetic testing, which is itself becoming increasingly sophisticated. Counselling in this context belongs to the cognitive end of the counselling spectrum and does not readily see itself as part of a psychotherapeutic process. It operates around a growing battery of genetic tests, the question of whether or not to test, and what decisions to make in the face of the results. Counsellors' agendas at the moment are to be informative about a genetic world they understand and want their clients to understand. The premise is the empowerment granted by information. The good outcome is understanding and a decision.

When faced with psychological problems, particularly those around living with the outcome of decisions acted upon, the counsellors refer on to psychotherapeutic resources. This situation presents an opportunity for genetic counsellors to develop greater awareness, skills and confidence in using counselling in genetics as a supportive, psychotherapeutic process as well as a cognitive decision-making one. In particular in the context of AD, when the actual genetic component is not so predictive, the need for a psychotherapeutic process and links with old-age psychiatry is highlighted.

References

Cull, A., Anderson, E.D.C., Campbell, S., Mackay, J., Smyth, E. and Steel, M. (1999) 'The impact of genetic counselling about breast cancer risk on women's risk perceptions and levels of distress', *British Journal of Cancer* **79**: 501–8.

Fraser, F.C. (1974) 'Genetic counselling', *American Journal of Human Genetics* **26**: 636–61.

Growdon, J.H. (1998) 'Apolipoprotein E and Alzheimer disease', *Archives of Neurology* **55**: 1053–4.

Hardy, J. (1996) 'New insights into the genetics of Alzheimer's disease', *Annals of Medicine* **28**: 255–8.

Harvey, R., Roques, P.K., Fox, N.C. and Rossor, M.N. (1998) 'CANDID – Counselling and Diagnosis in Dementia: a national telemedicine service supporting the care of younger patients with dementia', *International Journal of Geriatric Psychiatry* **13**: 381–8.

Lawson, K., Wiggins, S., Green, T., Adam, S., Bloch, M. and Hayden, M.R. (1996) 'Adverse psychological events occurring in the first year after predictive testing for Huntington's disease', *Journal of Medical Genetics* **33**: 856–62.

Lovestone, S. and Harper, P. (1994) 'Genetic tests and Alzheimer's disease', *Psychiatric Bulletin* **18**: 645.

Marteau, T. and Richards, M. (1996) *The Troubled Helix*, Cambridge: Cambridge University Press.

Marteau, T., Drake, H. and Bobrow, M. (1994) 'Counselling following diagnosis of a foetal abnormality: the differing approaches of obstetricians, clinical geneticists, and genetic nurses', *Journal of Medical Genetics* **31**: 864–67.

Michie, S., McDonald, V. and Marteau, T.M. (1997) 'Genetic counselling: information given, recall and satisfaction', *Journal of Patient Education and Counselling* **32**: 101–6.

Simpson, S.A. and Harding, A.E. (1993) 'Predictive testing for Huntington's disease: after the gene. The United Kingdom Huntington's Disease Prediction Consortium', *Journal of Medical Genetics* **30**: 1036–8.

Slooter, A.J.C. and van Duijn, C.M. (1997) 'Genetic epidemiology of Alzheimer disease', *Epidemiologic Reviews* **19**: 107–19.

van Zuuren, F.J., van Schie, E.C. and van Baaren, N.K. (1997) 'Uncertainty in the information provided during genetic counselling', *Journal of Patient Education and Counselling* **32**: 129–39.

Wiggins, S., Whyte, P., Huggins, M., Adam, S., Theilmann, J., Bloch, M., Sheps, S.B., Schechter, M.T. and Hayden, M.R. (1992) 'The psychological consequences of predictive testing for Huntington's disease: Canadian Collaborative Study of Predictive Testing', *New England Journal of Medicine* **327**: 1401–5.

Chapter 3

A psychodynamic counselling service for pregnant women

Mando Meleagrou

Introduction

This chapter charts the development of the psychotherapy consultation service for pregnant women at the Harris Birthright Research Centre for Fetal Medicine, a specialist unit at King's College Hospital London.[1]

The service emerged as a by-product of research[2] I was conducting into the psychology of pregnant women. In particular, I was trying to understand why some women who were told following a scan that they had very low probabilities of giving birth to Down's babies still went ahead with invasive tests which carried significant risks of miscarriage. It became apparent during this research just how powerful the feelings stirred up by pregnancy are. In particular, I understood that pregnant women are really grappling with two different babies: the one in their body and the one in their mind. Difficulties in distinguishing between the two seemed to be at the heart of the decision of some women to proceed with risky invasive tests.

Moreover, it was not just the subjects of my research who were struggling with intense emotions. I spent considerable time in the scan rooms to familiarise myself with the workings of the unit. It became clear to me that pregnant women – particularly those whose pregnancies were problematic and/or ended in terminations – were often in a state of extreme anxiety. There was a need for a psychotherapy service to help them.

Identifying the need was one thing. Setting up the service was another matter – not least because this was primarily a research unit. In particular, it was necessary to define the sort of treatment that was appropriate and persuade the professor of the unit and other medical staff of its need. Fortunately, this was possible because the doctors often found themselves on the receiving end of powerful emotions which they had neither the time nor the expertise to handle.

The service was set up in 1998. It focuses on women whose babies are dead or abnormal or whose pregnancies are, in other ways, problematic. Such women are alerted to the service by the doctors and midwives. They are offered six 1-hourly consultations and three follow-up appointments.

The service has shown significant potential. By the end of 1999, 140 women had been referred and 88 treated. Treatment helps women to reflect on what are traumatic events and the emotions they stir up. However, the service also has significant limitations. As a therapist working single-handedly, I have lacked the input of colleagues in helping define the best way to treat patients. Moreover, short-term treatment cannot properly explore the range of feelings unearthed during pregnancy.

Although the service is intended to help pregnant women, an unintended benefit has been the way it has helped the doctors and midwives deal with the powerful emotions swirling around the unit.

The background

I began working at the unit in 1996 as a psychotherapist research fellow on a project inspired by an intriguing phenomenon which brought to life contemporary psychoanalytic ideas (Britton, 1998). This phenomenon concerned some pregnant women's decision to have a diagnostic test (Chorionic Villus Sampling or CVS)[3] for fetal chromosomal abnormalities when their age-related risk of having a baby with Down's syndrome is significantly reduced by an ultrasound screening test (nuchal translucency scan).[4] While ultrasound screening provides a highly accurate prediction of the patient's likelihood of having an abnormal baby at birth, the diagnostic test provides conclusive evidence of whether the baby is abnormal. The women's decision would not have been so puzzling had it not been for the fact that their risk of having a miscarriage due to the diagnostic test is 1 per cent and this is often up to eight times higher than their predicted chance of having a baby with Down's.

This challenged the doctors' assumption that if patients were informed that their individual chance of having a baby with Down's was low they would opt against having a diagnostic test. It was instead clear to them that some of their patients were not sufficiently reassured by external medical evidence which suggested, rather than conclusively established, that their baby was normal whilst others could not tolerate the small uncertainty inherent in the probability that their baby was normal. Given all this, they realised that their patients' interpretation of their likelihood of having an abnormal baby was influenced by psychological factors about which they wanted to know more. This was the point at which the doctors' curiosity converged with my interest in examining the women's decision in terms of their fantasies about their unborn baby and their capacity to think reflectively.

Prior to starting my research, as I was familiar neither with the work of the unit nor the patients' experience of their examinations I decided to spend a few months observing in the scan rooms. It was then that I realised that my research concerned only a small minority of patients who were referred to the unit. Of the rest some patients had problem pregnancies such as intrauterine growth restriction (that is, the baby is not growing properly) which required regular monitoring and further investigations. Others needed to have further investigations because of an indication on their twenty-weeks' anomaly scan at their local hospital that their baby was most probably abnormal. In the case of some of these patients the outcome of their examinations showed that their babies had spina bifida or hydronephrosis (kidney problems) which is a marker for chromosomal abnormalities. In the case of other women, it showed that their babies had hydrocephalus (that is, excess fluid in the brain) and, depending on the amount of fluid in the baby's brain, some of them were told that their baby was already severely brain damaged. Furthermore a large number of patients discovered at the start of their ultrasound examination that their babies were already dead or that they had a serious defect. Others were told that their pregnancy was potentially complicated.

Despite the fact that the doctors and particularly the midwives responded sensitively to the patients' distress and anxiety, their input of sympathy and support was limited. This was not only because time and resources were scarce but more importantly because emotional comfort only partly met the patients' needs. The full nature of their need I was yet to understand but it was clear to me that the patients' visible pain did not fully reflect the impact on them of what had happened in their pregnancy. Similarly it was evident to me that the technological and scientific advances in fetal medicine had created a psychological vacuum and that the patients were not the only ones who suffered the emotional consequences.

The doctors and the midwives were recurrently at the receiving end of their patients' raw feelings, which they had no choice but to tolerate irrespective of the fact that they were disturbed themselves by the outcome of their patients' examinations. Parallel to this, the diversities inherent in their patients' perception of them was frequently the source of confusion and distress whilst the sheer number of patients they were seeing daily was in itself overwhelming.

As a result of my observations I grew confident that the provision of psychological help at the unit was not a luxury but a necessity. This was not only because the patients would benefit from it but also because the staff would be spared the dual responsibility of having to deal with the patients' medical and psychological needs. However, for this to materialise I knew that my medical colleagues had to recognise that there was no alternative but to include their patients' psychological needs in their medical care arrangements at the unit. The fact that they were already aware that their patients' psychological make-up was instrumental in their interpretation of their likelihood of having an abnormal baby was a promising starting point.

From past experience I also knew that the systematic and efficient provision of psychological help within a medical setting is subject to a number of practical issues that had to be addressed from the start. For example, I expected that the patients' clinical management would involve extensive liaison work with medical and mental health professionals who were not based at the unit. Particularly problematic in this respect was the fact that there were no mechanisms within the existing structure of the unit to facilitate my potential involvement with non-medical professionals.

I was also familiar with the hazards of needing to secure the regular use of a suitable room in which I could see my patients. As with other medical settings, space at the unit was not only limited but was also designed to accommodate the patients' medical needs and occupied because of them. Nevertheless I expected that once the patients' psychological needs were accorded the importance they deserved the apparent lack of physical space to cater for them would be less problematic.

The prospect of being the only psychotherapist on site was daunting, not only because of the practical but also because of the emotional implications of working in isolation. To secure the necessary support it was essential to forge close links with colleagues working at other settings locally and to ensure regular supervision.

Finally, given the constraints of the setting and the specific reasons for which patients were likely to seek psychological help, short-term therapeutic intervention was clearly the most appropriate type of psychoanalytically informed treatment to offer. However, what such intervention would actually involve I was yet to find out.

The development of the service

Early 1997, I had decided that a psychotherapy service was needed to support the medical and research work of the unit. But before such a service could be established four issues had to be resolved:

- a system for dealing with medical care had to be developed;
- the nature of the psychotherapy treatment had to be defined;
- a better understanding of the conflicts, anxieties and fantasies unearthed by pregnancy was needed;
- the doctors and midwives needed to be won over to the idea that a psychotherapy service would help their work.

Medical care

Given the probing nature of the two types of interviews[5] I was using in my project, I was concerned that my subjects, who were already in the throes of powerful feelings evoked by their pregnancy, would be further stirred up. In view of this I had to look into the patients' medical care arrangements at the unit in order to establish whom to liase with if any of my subjects requested or needed psychological support following their participation in the project.

As a result I discovered that, although the professor at the unit had overall medical responsibility for the patients' care and treatment, it was their GPs I had to liase with in relation to their psychological needs. Given this, and with my subjects' permission, I informed their GPs about the nature of the research project. I also brought to their attention the possibility of my having to liase with them in order to ensure the provision of further psychological support to those of my subjects who requested or needed this. By setting in place a structure within which my subjects' psychological needs could be properly addressed it was now possible to envisage a process by which some aspects of the patients' clinical management could be dealt with in conjunction with their GPs.

The type of treatment

I soon realised that the focus of both interviews captured my subjects' preoccupations and because of this they appreciated the opportunity to talk to an interested listener about what was most prominent in their mind.

This was particularly apparent in relation to one of the interviews, which included three conversations with my subjects to discuss their feelings, thoughts and anxieties about their pregnancy and their baby.

Even though these conversations were not intended to have a therapeutic value, they frequently did in the sense that they facilitated my subjects' capacity to think about their experience of being pregnant and to gain some insight into it. It was soon clear to me that my conversations with my subjects had turned into a form of short-term therapeutic intervention because of the combination of two factors: the psychoanalytically informed framework within which they were conducted and my subjects' receptive state of mind.

In light of this the type of short-term treatment I was planning to offer patients began to emerge in my mind.

The nature of the pregnant women's beliefs about their baby's health

Due to my conversations with my subjects I grew familiar with the ordinary conflicts, anxieties and fantasies that pregnancy unearths in its wake. Judging by what they said, the baby in their mind was the source of all sorts of beliefs they had about their baby's health and these influenced their expectations of the outcome of their examination. It was soon clear to me that my subjects' beliefs captured their fantasies (see Britton 1998) about their unborn baby and in particular its identification with aspects of them and/or their relationship with their partner that they feared were damaged or that they idealised or that they were yet to resolve. I also understood that during their ultrasound examination it was the baby in their mind who was tested against external evidence concerning the health of the baby in their body.

Given this, their interpretation of the outcome of their examination was largely influenced by the extent to which the baby in their mind was differentiated from the baby in their body. Those subjects who recognised that the source of their beliefs was none other than the baby in their mind were open to the possibility of discovering that their beliefs corresponded to or conflicted with the medical facts about their baby's health. As a result when the doctors told them that their baby was most probably normal they were sufficiently reassured.

By contrast, those of my subjects who believed that there was something wrong with their baby but did not recognise that this corresponded to their ideas rather than the facts (see Britton 1998) about their baby's well-being were not reassured by the doctors' findings. Instead, some of them maintained that what they believed about their baby's health was as valid as the doctors' findings since the latter corresponded to the doctors' observations rather than to concrete medical evidence concerning their baby's health. Some of them were indifferent to and others dismissive of the outcome of their examination. In view of this, the only option open to these women was to have a diagnostic test.

Furthermore it transpired that some of them could not tolerate any degree of uncertainty concerning their likelihood of having a baby with Down's because in their mind uncertainty was equated with bad news. As a result, the objectively small possibility that they might be the ones whose baby had Down's was viewed by them as a high probability.

Similarly, when confronted by medical evidence that their baby was abnormal, some patients said that they already knew something was wrong with their baby. Others disputed the credibility of the medical facts. Yet others said that they had hoped that the outcome of their examination would not have confirmed the dreaded possibility that all was not well with their baby.

Winning over the doctors and midwives

The doctors' aspiration to integrate their patients' medical and psychological needs converged with mine over the patients' anxiety prior to and after their examinations at the unit. The doctors were aware that the quality of the medical care they were striving to offer was frequently undermined by their failure properly to address the patients' anxiety about their examinations. For this reason they were eager to find ways of responding effectively to the patients' state of mind both prior to and after their examinations.

In the meantime, judging by what my subjects said, I understood that their examination was not the source but the catalyst of their anxieties about their baby's well-being. This concurred with my medical colleagues' observations that patients varied in terms of their anxiety about their examinations, and similarly some patients were more sceptical than others about the outcome of their examination. This suggested to them that patients had preconceived ideas about their baby's health which influenced not only their expectations concerning the outcome of their examination but also their interpretation of it.

In view of this, the doctors realised that there was nothing they could do to alleviate the patients' anxiety about their examinations but, concurrently with this, they also recognised that some aspects of their examinations often exacerbated the patients' anxiety. Given this, they appreciated that the best way forward was to prepare patients for their examinations by informing them what these involved and by acknowledging that what they were likely to experience would be unsettling. This prompted the publication of a leaflet which patients receive when they arrive at the unit.

Furthermore the doctors were aware that it was not sufficient that patients had the opportunity to discuss with them the outcome of their examination once this was completed because their queries and concerns continued to emerge long after they had left the unit. This prompted us to set up a 24-hour answerphone/helpline which patients can contact after their examinations and throughout their pregnancy if they have medical queries or need psychological help.

By contrast to our initial assumption, patients rarely contact the helpline to request psychological help and yet their distress or anxiety is often communicated through the specific nature of their medical queries. For example, many patients contact the helpline shortly after their nuchal translucency scan either because they do not understand what their chance of having an abnormal baby actually means or because they are not sufficiently reassured that all is most probably well with their baby. Of the patients in the second group some want to discuss the option of having a diagnostic test and others want the doctors to advise them as to whether they should have such a test. It is also common for patients to contact the helpline following an indication on their twenty-weeks' scan that their baby is probably abnormal or has a serious defect. Alternatively the patients' queries concern complications in late pregnancy or symptoms associated with an early or late miscarriage. The helpline messages are recorded in writing and subsequently allocated to various doctors, who deal with them at the end of each working day.

Due to the leaflet and helpline, the doctors were now firmly behind the idea of including the patients' psychological needs in their medical care arrangements at the unit. Meanwhile the midwives welcomed the idea of offering patients psychological help because they were aware that neither their friendly support nor their sympathetic understanding could remedy the deeply disturbing feelings stirred up by problem pregnancies. Particularly problematic in this respect was their involvement with patients, who were regularly reaching out to them for help because they were distressed due to ongoing complications in their pregnancy or their decision to terminate their abnormal pregnancy.

This was the background against which the previously remote prospect of setting up a psychological support service at the unit began emerging as a reality. In the first instance it was decided that priority should be accorded to the psychological needs of two groups of patients: those who discovered that their baby was dead or abnormal and those with problem pregnancies. This service started in 1998.

The baby in the mind: two case studies

At the age of 38 Mrs X was pregnant with her first baby. Her pregnancy was planned and very much wanted. Judging by what she said, her baby was identified in her mind with the special little girl she had once been to her parents and with the most loving aspects of her relationship with her husband. It was also clear that for Mrs X this was the baby she had always hoped she would have. Her reasons for thinking this were twofold: first, being the eldest of four girls she had helped her mother to look after her little sisters and to them she was their little mummy. Her involvement with her little sisters was the source of great pleasure in her life and, because of this, ever since she was a little girl she had longed to have her own baby and be a proper mother.

Second, three years before this pregnancy her marriage was on the verge of breaking up and she and her husband separated for a while. During their trial separation they managed to resolve some of their difficulties by talking to each other and by seeking professional help. Eighteen months later they were living together again and, although they both felt confident that their relationship was back on solid ground, it took them a while longer before they felt safe to resume their sexual relationship. She said that once this happened it consolidated in their mind the triumph of love and hope over despair and destruction. A year later, when they decided to have a baby, the baby she was yet to conceive was already in their minds the product of the most hopeful and creative aspects of their relationship. Due to this they decided that, if they had a baby girl, they would call her Hope.

Given all this it was not surprising that Mrs X thought that her pregnancy would progress smoothly and that her baby would be healthy and normal. As she herself put it: 'Deep down I always felt and I still feel that my baby is fine.' For this reason when at the start of her pregnancy the doctors were concerned that it was ectopic, she was worried but also hopeful that 'all would turn out to be fine'.

Nevertheless Mrs X was also aware that neither the outcome of her pregnancy nor the physical well-being of her baby was dependent on the way she felt and the thoughts she had. In view of this she was concerned that, given her age, her risk of having a baby with Down's was relatively high.

Initially she thought that in order to establish that her baby was normal she had no other option but to have a diagnostic test (amniocentesis) at twenty weeks. Even though she did not want to have a baby with Down's, at the same time the prospect of having a diagnostic test worried her because she knew that this could result in a miscarriage.

Given her dilemma, she was hugely relieved to discover that it was possible to have a non-invasive ultrasound screening test (nuchal translucency scan) to establish her individual chance of having a baby with Down's. Prior to her nuchal translucency scan Mrs X and her husband decided that they would not consider the option of having an invasive test unless the outcome of her examination indicated that her predicted chance of having a baby with Down's was higher than her age-related risk. In their view it was unwise to opt for a test due to which her risk of having a miscarriage would be higher than her predicted chance of having an abnormal baby at birth.

In the process of exploring the way she felt and the thoughts she had prior to her nuchal translucency scan, it transpired that although Mrs X did not know what to expect she was confident that all was well with her baby. As she herself put it: 'The only thing I knew was that deep down I felt that my baby was normal and healthy. If something, I had expected the doctors to tell me that my baby was OK. But, as I waited for my turn, I saw many women coming out of the scan rooms in tears and I kept hoping that I would not be one of them. We were like the last ones to be seen and I was anxious and I kept telling myself that as long as they said that my chance of having a baby with Down's was not higher than my age risk I would be happy.' When I asked her whether she knew what her age-related risk of having a baby with Down's was she replied: 'Yes, and this was the only thing I knew for a fact. It was 1:150.'

The outcome of Mrs X's examination indicated a five-fold reduction of her age-related risk of having a baby with Down's to 1:770. This meant that had she decided to have a diagnostic test her risk of having a miscarriage (1:100) would have been more than seven times higher than her predicted chance of having a baby with Down's. Mrs X was relieved by the outcome of her examination and as she herself put it: 'I felt so happy, I was in tears. I do not know whether I was crying because I was relieved or because I saw our baby on the screen. I think it was a bit of both. I could not believe that what we had just seen on the screen was our baby and I had not expected my risk of having a baby with Down's to be reduced as much as it did. I remember walking out of your centre feeling so relieved.'

Following the outcome of her examination Mrs X did not simply think that given the odds it would have been unwise to have a diagnostic test. Instead, once she saw her baby on the scan she realised that she could not subject it to a potentially damaging procedure for no good reason. In her mind this would have been the same as inflicting damage on her helpless baby. She also felt that it was easier to put up with the fact that she did not know for sure that her baby was normal than with the thought of having a test that could have harmed her baby.

As she herself put it: 'I could not live with the guilt of harming my baby but I can live with the uncertainty that my baby might be the one who has Down's. The way I look at it is that nothing is certain in pregnancy and for that matter nothing is certain in our life. Nothing is within my control and there are so many things that could go wrong in my pregnancy and having a baby with Down's is only one of them. A friend of mine lost her baby two days before it was due to be born and they could not even tell her why her baby died. I also know that there are a number of other abnormalities that my baby could have and I could spend the whole of my pregnancy worrying about this and everything else that could go wrong. And I do worry but I also know that there is nothing I could do to stop bad things from happening. The best I can do is to hope that I will have my baby and it will be healthy.'

In the course of our conversations Mrs X's capacity to think reflectively was also apparent in relation to other aspects of her past and current life circumstances. For example, she had little difficulty in recognising that being her sister's little mummy had been the source not only of pleasure but also of resentment. Similarly she acknowledged that her picture of motherhood was largely idealised and that the prospect of being a mother was already the source of considerable conflict. Furthermore it was clear that although her baby felt known and real to her she was none the less aware that she had yet to find out who her baby really was.

At the age of 38 Mrs Y had a six-year-old son and was pregnant with her second child. Her pregnancy, like Mrs X's, was also planned but in her mind this was the baby she was never meant to have. Initially I understood that this was due to the fact that shortly before she became pregnant she had given up hoping that she would ever have a second child because her husband was hostile to the idea. When her husband changed his mind she was concerned that this would be short-lived and for this reason she decided to try to get pregnant straight away. When, contrary to her expectations, she became pregnant within a month she was pleasantly surprised but also fearful that she would have a miscarriage. Furthermore, judging by what she said, I also understood that from the start of her pregnancy the baby in her body was pictured in her mind as special but also doomed.

Given all this, on the one hand she was thrilled to be pregnant but, on the other, she was constantly worried that something would go wrong or that her baby would be abnormal. Unlike Mrs X, she did not recognise that neither the outcome of her pregnancy nor the well-being of her baby were dependent on what she felt and the thoughts she had. Instead what she already believed about her baby's physical well being was further confirmed in her mind by the fact that her risk of having an abnormal baby was relatively high because of her age and similarly her pregnancy was more likely to be complicated. Given all this, Mrs Y was determined to have a diagnostic test to establish that her baby was normal and it transpired that her husband was adamant that she should do this.

Unlike Mrs X, she was relieved to discover that it was possible to have a diagnostic test (CVS) early in her pregnancy and had the nuchal translucency scan not been part of her routine prenatal care at her local hospital she would not have considered this option. Like Mrs X, prior to her nuchal translucency scan Mrs Y said that she was anxious but by contrast to Mrs X she had expected that the doctors would tell her that there was something wrong with her baby. When the outcome of her examination indicated a five-fold reduction of her age-related risk of having a baby with Down's, Mrs Y was not relieved but instead she was partly dismissive and partly mistrustful of the doctors' findings.

As she herself put it: 'It meant nothing to me that my chance of having a baby with Down's was 1:770. This was just a number, a statistic that the doctors came up with. What if they were wrong? What if I was the one woman whose baby had Down's? I could not go through my pregnancy believing this and do nothing about it. I don't know why, but I really thought that there was something wrong with this baby. I just had to know that my baby was normal. Besides, I had my son to think of. It would not have been fair on him to have a sister or a brother who had Down's. Once we are dead and gone it would have been his responsibility to look after his sibling. I could not do this to him. It would not have been right to have inflicted this burden on him.'

The fact that her risk of having a miscarriage due to the diagnostic test was now seven times higher than her predicted chance of having a baby with Down's did not deter her from going ahead with the test. Instead, she thought that for the sake of knowing that her baby was normal this was a risk worth taking. None the less, Mrs Y, unlike most of the other women who thought the same, was also guilty for subjecting her baby to a potentially damaging procedure. As she herself put it: 'When I saw my baby on the scan my stomach churned at the thought of doing something that could have harmed it. When the needle went in I felt guilty for doing this to my baby. But then again had I not had the test and discovered at birth that my baby had Down's I would have felt guilty for bringing into the world a child who would have had no proper place in it. And I would have felt guilty for inflicting on my son the responsibility of being his brother's or sister's long-term carer.'

Like the rest of the women in the same group, in justifying her decision to have a diagnostic test Mrs Y communicated to me her failure to differentiate between the baby in her mind who was abnormal and the baby in her body who was most probably normal. Her failure to recognise that what she believed about her baby's health captured not the facts but her ideas about her baby was reflected in her interpretation of her likelihood of having a baby with Down's. In her mind, the small possibility that she would have been the one woman whose baby had Down's was a probability.

In the course of our conversations I understood that the primary source of Mrs Y's belief that she was never meant to have a second baby was not the background to her pregnancy but instead her early childhood fantasies about her mother's second pregnancy. Judging by what she said, it was clear that as a little girl Mrs Y, who was an only child until the age of six, had a fantasy that she was the only child her parents had wanted to have. For this reason when she was a little girl she believed that her parents were not meant to have another baby. Even though she joked that her parents 'betrayed' her by having a second child, her unjustified concerns that the news of her pregnancy had angered and upset her son suggested to me that this was how she had felt as a little girl about her mother's second pregnancy.

Given Mrs Y's identification with her son it seemed to me that her current belief that she was not meant to have a second baby stemmed from the little girl's fantasy that she was the only child her parents had ever wanted to have. At the same time, by identification with her mother her pregnancy was now at the mercy of the little girl's wrath and hence Mrs Y's anxiety that she would have a miscarriage or that something would go wrong in her pregnancy.

Judging by her current picture of her younger sister I was left with the impression that in the little girl's mind the baby her mother was never meant to have was turned into the 'wrong baby'. As she put it: 'Ever since she was a little girl she was the odd one out in our family and to this date she brings nothing but trouble and worry to the rest of us. She isn't like the rest of us. She is different. It is like she was born into the wrong family.'

It was also clear that over the years none of the negative feelings evoked by her sister's birth had lost their momentum. Her critical remarks about her sister's life style communicated intense envy and hostility whilst her rivalry was most powerfully brought forth by her portrait of herself as the impeccable daughter. At the same time, ever since she was a little girl Mrs Y had unrealistic concerns about her sister's well-being and this suggested to me that in her mind her sister was at risk of being damaged. Given the way she felt towards her sister, it seemed to me that the source of her fantasy was none other than her damaging feelings towards her. As a result she was also persecuted by guilt and this was communicated through her exaggerated sense of responsibility for her little sister's well-being and this also dated back to her early childhood.

All this led to my understanding that, by identification with her younger sister, the baby that Mrs Y was never meant to have was also the 'wrong baby' and at the mercy of her damaging feelings. The first was the source of Mrs Y's belief that her baby was abnormal and the second was the source of her irrational worries about her baby's health and safety after its birth.

Even though Mrs Y was not aware that her picture of her baby was coloured by her personal history, she was in no doubt that her husband's longstanding belief that 'a second baby was a recipe for trouble' stemmed from his history as an only child. Her understanding was that her husband's hostility to the idea of having a second baby reflected the way he had once felt about his parents having a second child. In her view this was further evidenced by the fact that her husband could not appreciate that their son wanted to have a sibling, because in the husband's mind by being an only child the son was already better off.

At some point it transpired that her husband shared her anxiety that their baby was abnormal and it was because of this that he had insisted that she should have a diagnostic test. In view of this I seized the opportunity to put across to her my understanding that she and her husband shared between them the idea that a second baby was the source of trouble and worry. Following on from this we were able to explore the meaning that her second baby had for her, and it was in the process of doing this that she began to appreciate that her picture of her baby was also coloured by her personal history. Similarly she began to realise that her anxiety about their baby's physical well-being, just like her husband's, stemmed from her ideas about their baby.

The structure of the service

Referrals

Initially the two main sources of referrals were the professor and the midwives at the unit because they each have follow-up contact with patients whose pregnancy is either terminated because of fetal chromo-somal abnormalities or is complicated and requires monitoring or surgical intervention. Individual patients and couples who request or are actively seeking psychological help are automatically referred to the service and the rest are informed of its existence.

Gradually, as the rest of the doctors became aware that the option of offering patients psychological help was now available, they also began to refer patients who they thought would appreciate or need psychological help following a bad examination outcome.

Finally, in liaison with the bereavement midwife on the labour ward, those of our patients whose baby has died in late pregnancy or during labour due to medical or unexplained reasons are also offered the option of being referred to the service. Within a week of being referred to the service all patients are contacted by telephone and offered a first appointment.

Treatment

Given my understanding that the most appropriate type of psychoana-lytically informed treatment was short-term intervention, patients were initially offered six weekly therapeutic consultations (Garland 1998) each lasting one hour. Hence, the service was now called the Psychotherapy Consultation Service.

The aim of the consultations is threefold:

1   to give patients the opportunity to talk to an understanding and sympathetic listener about what has happened in their pregnancy;
2   to facilitate the patients' capacity to think about what has happened in their pregnancy;
3   to facilitate the long and complicated process of mourning what and who was lost by the outcome of the pregnancy.

Although the outcome of the patient's pregnancy is central to the consultations, as with all psychoanalytic clinical work, the consultations are not structured around specific themes and the therapist follows rather than leads the patient and provides no specific directions. Instead, emphasis is put on what emerges in the course of each consultation and the attempt is made to understand what this communicates about the patient's internal experience of what happened.

Soon after I began seeing patients, it became apparent to me that for some patients the consultations marked the beginning of a process which they wanted or needed to continue. For others the consultations were sufficient help, and yet most of these patients thought that it was important to have the option of coming back to see me should they need further psychological help in the future.

All this prompted me to offer all patients three follow-up appointments arranged at six-weekly intervals from their last consultation and the option to be referred on for further treatment at an appropriate setting local to them. Patients are informed that following their last consultation they can request to be referred on for further treatment at any point.

However, it was soon evident to me that there were two groups of patients whose needs could not be accommodated within the existing structure of the service. One group included those patients who were pregnant again shortly after the loss of their baby. Having previously thought that the consultations had been sufficient help, these were now requesting more psychological help. The other group included patients with complicated or abnormal pregnancies who, following the completion of their consultations, requested or needed more help.

In the process of making the necessary arrangements I realised that by the time the patients' referral was properly considered their pregnancy would have been either completely or nearly over. Given this I had no option but to offer these patients the choice of having short-term psychotherapy or further follow-up appointments with me for the rest of their pregnancy. Following the birth of their baby such patients are also offered four follow-up appointments arranged at three-monthly intervals and the option to be referred on for further treatment.

Liaison work with other professionals

This includes the patients' GPs, the medical staff and the midwives at the unit and other mental health professionals who are based outside the unit.

General practitioners

Following the patient's permission her GP is informed about her referral to the service and the type of treatment on offer. When necessary the patient's referral for further treatment is dealt with in liaison with her GP, and the same applies if she needs to be assessed by a psychiatrist or hospitalised during or after her consultations.

The medical staff and midwives at the unit

The professor at the unit is also informed about the patient's referral to the service and, following the completion of her consultations, about her referral for further treatment. Furthermore, with the patient's permission he is also made aware of her concerns about the medical aspects of her current or future pregnancy. These are subsequently discussed either when the patient is next seen for her routine examination at the unit or at her postnatal consultation. When necessary I attend the patient's postnatal consultation with the view to offering any patient who has not been referred to the service the opportunity to voice her feelings and thoughts about what had happened in her pregnancy.

My involvement with the doctors covers two main areas: (a) their referrals to the service, which gives us the opportunity to discuss their experiences with patients. This has contributed to and continues to inform my understanding of the psychological implications that their work has for them; (b) we deal with the patients' queries on the helpline and this gives me the opportunity to learn from the doctors about the medical aspects of pregnancy.

From the start the midwives were particularly keen to talk to me about their involvement with two groups of patients: those with problem pregnancies and those who turned to them for psychological support but were not willing or suitable to be referred to the service. As a result my understanding of the emotional impact on the staff of the patients' traumatic experiences was further enhanced. Concurrently with this my regular discussions with the midwives contributed to forging a close working relationship with them. Particularly important in this respect was the midwives' help in overcoming some of the practical hurdles I had anticipated in relation to the daily running of the service. I also benefited from their liaison work with their colleagues on the labour ward because it was this that paved the way for bringing the existence of the service to their attention. This in turn secured the referral to the service of patients whose need for psychological help had previously been hard to meet.

My liaison work with my medical colleagues and the midwives was instrumental in facilitating and consolidating the integration of the service within the medical structure of the unit. It was because of this that other medical and non-medical professionals who are not based at the unit but are involved with the patients' prenatal and postnatal care became aware of the existence of the service within a relatively short period of time.

Mental health professionals

Given that a large number of patients who are referred to the service come from different parts of the country, their referral for further treatment involves extensive liaison work with a number of mental health professionals. Depending on what is available locally, patients are referred for counselling or ongoing psychotherapy to their local or district hospital, specialist units or centres and GP surgeries. Alternatively patients are referred to their community midwife or to the clinical psychologists or psychiatric social workers at their local hospital who offer them further psychological support. Frequently the funding for the patients' treatment involves extensive liaison work with hospital trust managers and other professionals working for the local health authority. When the provision of psychological help is not available locally and provided that the patients can fund their own treatment they are referred to private psychotherapists.

The potentials and limitations of the service

The demand for the service and the lack of resources

During its first 2 years, the service received 140 referrals. Of these, fifty-two failed to attend their first appointment or did not take up the offer to be seen. Of those who did attend, fifty-five attended all six consultations and thirty-three attended between one and five consultations.

The number of referrals and the patients' uptake of treatment suggest that a previously unmet need at the unit was correctly identified and responded to by the systematic provision of psychological help. This is further confirmed by the patients' feedback about the service and the increasing number of referrals from professionals based outside the unit who are involved with the patients' antenatal and postnatal care.

However, the fact that the service was set up and is run single-handedly is a major limitation. The lack of input from other colleagues has implications not only for the provision of treatment but also for the structure and daily running of the service. For example, in setting the objectives of the therapeutic consultations the input of colleagues with the relevant clinical experience would have been more appropriate than my background in individual psychotherapy. Similarly, issues such as the suitability of referrals, the patients' clinical management and future treatment cannot be properly considered or dealt with by a single psychotherapist.

For example, the time-consuming nature of my liaison work with other professionals further limits my availability as a clinician but more importantly it interferes with my relationship with my patients. Similarly the way the patients' need for psychological help is currently screened does not exclude the referral of borderline patients. Often, such patients are more unsettled than helped by my intervention and the arising consequences are problematic not only for me but also for the rest of the staff. Furthermore, patients whose pregnancy is not the cause of medical concerns but the source of ordinary and yet difficult feelings and conflicts are less likely to receive the psychological help they may need. Also problematic is ensuring that those of my patients who may need support during my absence receive this. For this I currently rely on the patients' GPs or the professor and the midwives at the unit. Apart from being unsatisfactory, such arrangements are inevitably experienced as burdensome by the relevant professionals.

Finally, as I had expected, being the only psychotherapist on site is an isolating experience and for this reason regular supervision is particularly important because it provides me with a supportive structure; on the one hand, by being the source of theoretical input regular supervision enhances my understanding of my patients' emotional and mental state; on the other, by creating a space where I can talk about the emotional impact on me of my patients' traumatic experiences it enables me to sustain my capacity to think about these experiences instead of simply feeling overwhelmed by them.

The efficacy and limitations of the therapeutic consultations

The patients who are seen by the service share between them four common features, all of which are relevant to the efficacy and the limitations of the therapeutic consultations.

The first common feature is the breakdown of their capacity to cope with what had happened in their pregnancy and its aftermath. It is for this reason that most patients seek or are referred for psychological help. In the case of some patients their need for psychological help is met by the very fact that the service exists. As a result some of them idealise the kind of help on offer and once the consultations begin they are deeply disappointed to discover that these are not a panacea for their difficulties. For this reason some of them stop attending. Of those who continue, only a few are able to recognise within the confines of a limited intervention that the consultations have failed to match their expectations. Provided that they are able to reflect on their disappointment in the consultations they begin to appreciate that no kind of help or support can eradicate the loneliness inherent in their struggle to reconcile themselves with what has happened. This in turn lessens their disappointment in their friends and relatives for failing to provide them with the support they need and enables them to benefit from their sympathy and understanding.

Similarly, prior to the start of the consultations some patients are convinced that no kind of help can make a difference to the way they feel and others are doubtful that it would. The extent to which such patients are open and receptive to what is on offer determines whether their preconceived ideas are either challenged by their experience or confirmed by the fact that the therapeutic consultations can only partly meet their needs.

The efficacy of the therapeutic consultations is also overestimated by some of the doctors and midwives. This is because in their mind the patients' psychological needs are automatically met by the fact that the relevant help is available to them. Furthermore, many of them under-estimate the limitations of a short-term therapeutic intervention because they do not fully appreciate that the patients' traumatic experiences have serious long-term consequences for which further help is often necessary.

The second common feature emerges at the start of the consultations and concerns the impact on the patients of a traumatic event, which was directly related to their pregnancy. Even though, depending on the patients' medical circumstances, the particular events vary, what is confirmed by it in reality does not. This corresponds to the patients' worst fears, deepest anxieties and most frightening fantasies about the inside of their body as a damaged or a damaging place and about their baby's well-being. It is the convergence of psychic and external reality that renders the particular event traumatic and consequently such an event is overwhelming and incapacitating and cannot be managed psychically (Garland 1998).

In view of this, the therapeutic consultations initially meet the patients' urgent need to communicate the impact on them of what has happened. For example, some patients begin their consultations by bringing forth the flood of overwhelming feelings unearthed by the traumatic event or by voicing the fears, anxieties and fantasies that this has confirmed in reality. Alternatively some patients begin by saying that they do not know where to start and by this they usually mean that they feel lost inside because their mind is flooded with overwhelming feelings. Furthermore, others begin by saying that what happened makes no sense to them or by giving a detailed and graphic account of the actual facts. In the case of some patients this communicates their attempt to put some kind of structure to an experience yet to be assimilated in their mind. In the case of others the impact on them of the particular traumatic event is brought across vividly by their account of what actually happened.

At the same time the presence of a sympathetic listener such as the therapist provides most patients with the experience of someone who is open and receptive to what they say but, unlike them, is not unduly overwhelmed by its emotional impact. Instead, what is unearthed/evoked inside the therapist contributes to his/her understanding of the patients' state of mind (Garland 1998). It is this particular way of being listened to that provides most patients from the start of the consultations with an experience of being understood and consequently of being contained (Garland 1998). Both of these are particularly important because they correspond precisely to what the patients feel is no longer available from within themselves. As one patient put it: 'Ever since that time [the traumatic event in her pregnancy] I feel that there is nothing left inside me to hold me together. I feel that what held me together all my life is now gone, lost.'

In psychoanalytic terms this reflects the patients' internal experience of the traumatic event. The latter is understood to be an experience of being abandoned by loving, good internal objects which protect and contain and instead being left to the mercy of hateful and hating objects felt to have caused the trauma (Garland, 1998). The second is often captured by the patients' fear that more misfortunes will befall them or those who are close to them. Given these patients' psychological circum- stances, it is inevitable that many of them are inclined to idealise a good experience of being understood and contained. Similarly, others are mistrustful or even fearful of the therapist, who is viewed as a potentially damaging rather than a helpful figure.

Whichever the case, it is difficult within the confines of a short-term therapeutic intervention to address properly the patients' transference. This is not only because there is not enough time to do this but also because it takes time for patients to appreciate the depth of their relationship with the therapist.

Particularly problematic, in this respect, is my patients' tendency to spare me the anger and disappointment provoked by my failure to 'make things better' for them. This has two implications. First, the patients' idealisation of the therapist limits the extent to which it is possible in the course of the consultations to help them to begin to face the negative feelings provoked by the hoped-for baby's physical reality. Amongst other things their attempt to preserve the therapist as the source only of goodness captures their difficulty in acknowledging that the baby they had hoped for is not only the source of their love but also of their troubles. Second, by sparing both the therapist and the baby they had hoped for their anger and disappointment, they direct their negative feelings towards other suitable targets – for example, the medical professionals who are often blamed for what has happened. This in turn can create tensions between the therapist and the medical professionals who are involved in the patients' care.

Similarly, when the therapist is viewed as a potentially damaging rather than a helpful figure the patients' reluctance to recognise this is also problematic. My understanding is that my patients' picture of me as someone who is potentially damaging largely reflects their fear that my intervention would bring to light what they feel is damaged inside them, which in their mind corresponds to what has caused the damage to their baby. Unless they can acknowledge this, it is not possible to help them to bring forth, let alone gain insight into, their fears that they are to blame for their baby's physical predicament. As a result some of these patients end their consultations prematurely and only a few of those who continue begin to bring forth their fears that the source of damage to their baby is inside them. For the rest such fears are simply the source of persecution throughout their consultations.

Provided that the therapist's attempt to make contact with the patients is successful, as the consultations progress their experience of being understood and contained enables them to begin to recover their capacity to think about what had happened. It is at this point that the third common feature – their experience of being pregnant – becomes apparent. The fact that most of these patients were already exposed inside to the primitive fears, anxieties and fantasies that are normally unearthed at the point of impact with the traumatic event makes it easier for the therapist to access all this in them. Similarly most of these patients are more than usually aware of the kind of figures that inhabit their internal world and their ways of relating to each other because these correspond to the different aspects of them with which the baby in their body was already identified in their mind.

As a result they, just like my research subjects, are exceptionally receptive to an approach that aims at understanding the impact on them of what has happened in terms of who they are as individuals and of who the baby in their body was in their mind. It is for this reason that within the space of six consultations many of them begin to make some sense of the impact on them of what happened in their pregnancy and a previously mind-blowing event begins to assume its particular meaning for them. Concurrently with this, the experience of making sense with someone else of what has happened to them enables many of them to begin to re-establish inside what they previously felt they had lost: an internal world in which good objects feel stronger and more reliable.

And yet the fact that most of these patients are in touch with what is normally defended against highlights the limitations of a short-term therapeutic intervention because what they bring forth cannot be properly explored or understood. For example, at best in the course of the consultations some patients begin to recognise that what they believed about their baby's health had no bearing on their baby's physical well-being. Even though this clears the way for exploring the baby in their mind which in turn brings forth their ideas about themselves or about their relationship or about the inside of their body, none of these can be examined in depth. As a result our understanding of what they feel is damaged inside them or alternatively of their fear to acknowledge this is incomplete and because of this their beliefs about their baby's health are only partly recognised for what they are. This is evident during their follow-up appointments, which are often dominated by their struggle to come to terms with the fact that their baby's physical reality was independent of what they had believed about its well-being.

Furthermore, given the short-term nature of my intervention and these patients' uninhibited flow of feelings, conflicts, anxieties and fantasies, striking the right balance between what needs to be addressed and what is best left intact can also be problematic. This is particularly relevant to my work with couples for whom their 'damaged' baby becomes the catalyst of the long-standing 'abnormalities' in their relationship. On the one hand, what they feel is damaged about their relationship needs to be addressed because in their mind their baby was from the start the product of a damaged or a damaging relationship. On the other hand, the difficulties in their relationship cannot be accorded the attention they deserve because this could expose them to what they could only begin to work on if they were offered long-term help. Given this, the consultations are at best the catalyst for the couple's decision to seek further treatment.

Finally, the fourth common feature is that they have all experienced a loss. In the case of some patients this is the baby they had hoped for, and in the case of others what they lose is the hope of ever repairing, by producing a healthy baby, what they feel is damaged inside them or in their relationship.

The efficacy and limitations of the therapeutic consultations are further illuminated by the extent to which they can facilitate the capacity of patients to mourn their lost baby. By creating a space where the outcome of their pregnancy can be thought about, the consultations contribute to these patients' recognition that inherent in the loss of the baby they had hoped for is the loss of what their baby had represented for them. In the case of some patients this corresponds to the loss of their ideas about the kind of life they would have had or the kind of parents they would have been. In the case of others it corresponds to the loss of the most loving and creative aspects of them or their relationship. It is in this context that the loss of the baby they had hoped for begins to emerge as the source not only of their grief but also of their anger and disturbing thoughts. As a result most of them begin to appreciate that 'coming to terms', as they themselves put it, with the loss of the baby they had hoped for involves facing not only the painful but also the angry and disturbing feelings provoked by it.

By creating a setting in which patients feel sufficiently safe, the therapeutic consultations facilitate the patients' capacity to acknowledge what they are already aware of but dare not admit: that their loss includes not only the baby they had hoped for but also the baby they were pregnant with. It is by recognising this that they begin to face the guilt, regrets and doubts provoked by their decision to have a termination and, because of this, the baby they were pregnant with begins to emerge as the source not only of badness but also of love and sadness. Similarly, by beginning to face the frightening ideas provoked by their baby's death they begin to feel less persecuted by their guilt for inflicting damage on their baby and the latter, instead of being a menacing figure in their mind, begins to emerge as a more vulnerable one.

All this, however, marks only the beginning of the long and complicated process of mourning which many patients have difficulties in pursuing once the consultations are completed. Short of receiving further help, many of them try to 'get on with their life', as they themselves put it, by 'pushing their pain, guilt and anger to the back of their mind'. Frequently in order to fill the emptiness left by the loss of their baby they conceive a new baby. In such cases, the ghost of the lost baby haunts their next pregnancy. This is a recurrent theme in the therapy of patients who lose a baby and continue to see me during their next pregnancy.

Notes

1   The Harris Birthright Centre for fetal medicine was set up in 1984 through the generosity of Sir Philip Harris and the charity organisation Birthright. Since that time it has developed into a major research and clinical unit for

fetal diagnosis and treatment. Each year more than 15,000 patients who are referred to the centre by their GPs or local hospitals benefit from its services and up to 100 doctors, midwives and scientists visit to observe its clinical activities and participate in research. The medical staff includes the Professor, 3 consultants and up to 40 medical research fellows. There are 3 midwives, 1 health psychologist research fellow and 1 psychotherapist.

2   I am yet to complete the research I was conducting and this chapter includes only my preliminary understanding of some of my qualitative interviews (dynamic conversations) with my subjects.

3   Chorionic villus sampling (CVS) involves the examination of chorionic villi (placenta fragments). Both baby and the placenta (afterbirth) develop from the same cell and so the chromosomes present in the cells of the placenta can be used to check the chromosomes of the baby. A woman who undergoes a CVS receives local anaesthetic and a fine needle is then passed into the uterus through the abdomen. A sample of chorionic villi is taken. The needle is carefully watched with an ultrasound scan to ensure it does not injure the fetus. The whole procedure takes 2–3 minutes and afterwards the fetal heart beat is checked that is normal. This test carries a 1 per cent risk of miscarriage.

4   The nuchal translucency scan is a first trimester (11–14 weeks) ultrasound scan which is carried through the abdomen. During the scan the size of the fetus is measured and major problems are identified. At the same time, the fluid behind the neck of the baby is measured. By combining the risk based on the woman's age, with information from the scan it is possible to predict her individual risk of having a baby with chromosomal abnormalities at birth.

   In fetuses with chromosomal abnormalities, cardiac defects and many genetic syndromes nuchal translucency is increased. A low risk reading on the nuchal translucency scan does not completely exclude the possibility of a chromosomal abnormality.

5   The research interviews consisted of two parts: (i) The Adult Attachment Interview, which is a structured interview that consists of 18 questions, all of which are structured around the topic of attachment. The focus of the interview is the individual's relationship with their mother and father during childhood. The emphasis is on the individual's ability to think, reflect and organise his/her mind in relation to early experiences and their influence on their adult personality. This interview is tape-recorded and transcribed verbatim; (ii) Three dynamic conversations.

Acknowledgements

I am deeply indebted to Dr Ron Britton, psychoanalyst, for helping me through his work and otherwise to understand the role and function of pregnant women's beliefs about their unborn baby. I am also grateful to him for his encouragement and support in setting up in the Psychotherapy Consultation Service at the centre and for suggesting the name for it.

   I am grateful to Mrs Elizabeth Spillius, psychoanalyst, whose weekly supervision of my clinical work has and continues to enrich my understanding of my patients' experiences whilst providing me with the supportive structure that I need in order *to do my work*.

I want to thank Margot Waddell, psychoanalyst, Dr Matthew Patrick, psychoanalyst and Professor Michael Rustin for their contribution to my work as a researcher.

Neither the Psychotherapy Consultation Service nor my research would have materialised had it not been for Professor Kypros Nicolaides who gave me the opportunity to work at the centre and develop my ideas. I am also grateful to the senior midwife, Pat Sorahaindo and to my medical colleagues, Dr Neil Sabire, Dr Athena Souka, Dr Chara Skentos, Dr Nikos Kametas, Dr Victoria Heath and Dr Caroline Paul for their unflagging support and unfailing commitment to the Help-Line.

Finally, I want to thank Hugo Dixon and Eleni Meleagrou for reading and editing many versions of this chapter; Dr Sue Davison for her comments and Peter Thomas for being a supportive editor.

Bibliography

Britton, R. (1998) 'Belief and psychic reality', in *Belief and Imagination*, London: Routledge.

Garland, C. (ed.) (1998) *Understanding Trauma: A Psychoanalytical Approach*, London: Duckworth.

Chapter 4

Nurse-led counselling in a renal unit

Amanda Logan

Introduction

This chapter describes how a renal unit in a busy teaching hospital functioned before the counselling service was set up, and explores the change in culture that has developed since the service has been in operation. It outlines some of the difficulties encountered whilst setting up the service, including both practical and ethical issues. It explores how the counselling service reflects some of the personal anxieties amongst the staff. I illustrate these issues using examples of work with patients with chronic illness, those undergoing dialysis treatments and families preparing for living-related transplantation. In addition, I examine the role and value of supervision.

The background

In 1988 I was employed as a ward sister on a renal intensive care unit. I was part of a team striving for medical excellence, which was involved in pioneering work in renal dialysis and transplantation. Typically patients would be admitted when they were critically ill with renal failure and its complications. They would be subjected to uncomfortable and invasive investigations, surrounded by machines and monitors and then, when their condition was stable, they would be informed by the doctors that they would henceforth require long-term haemodialysis or a kidney transplant. This news would often be imparted during a ward round when pressure of time and lack of privacy meant that the patient had no opportunity to share his or her shock and horror with the doctors.

The task of helping patients and their families come to terms with a diagnosis that implied profound changes in their future lives fell to the nurses on the ward. They frequently felt they were required to carry the lion's share of the emotional burden of this work without really having the time, skill or authority to do it. In many cases it became clear that after the initial shock patients become detached or even denied the unbearable reality of their condition and were then unable to take in any more information. It was often necessary to repeat simple instructions or even the basic facts several times. Some patients would remain in a prolonged state of denial which impaired their ability to take responsibility for managing their diet, fluid balance and dialysis regime. In this situation, a patient was often labelled as 'non-compliant' and subsequently forfeited professional sympathy and support during a difficult period in his or her life.

More commonly patients would react to the dawning reality of their condition with grief and helplessness. After the initial relief that they were alive and could be kept alive with haemodialysis came the realisation of what this meant: the construction of an arterio-venous fistula, which can be unsightly and difficult to disguise; the absolute requirement to attend hospital three days a week and to be attached to a dialysis machine for several hours each time; the careful attention to diet, salt and fluid restrictions; the lethargy of chronic anaemia; the curtailment of future possibilities at work or in sport and other leisure pursuits; changes in the family structure with the new role as the sick one in need of protection and support; loss of libido and a poor body image; all these confront patients with their mortality, some for the first time.

In response to these deprivations, it is unsurprising that depression, anger and resentment directed at the medical team are almost normal. The inability to cope with feelings of anger would often result in indirect self-harm, such as ignoring a fluid restriction in an attempt to deny the loss of control of their lives.

Over time it became increasingly clear to some members of the team that the failure to give proper attention to the psychological needs of our patients affected them adversely. At the same time public awareness of the importance of psychological care for those with chronic illness was evident in greater coverage of the issues in the national press. By a happy coincidence my interest in setting up a counselling service was met by a service manager who was keen to support new ventures. I was released from my duties as a ward sister and given a six-month contract on the nursing budget to pilot my ideas. One period of six months led to another as the value of the work became ever more apparent.

The early days

The first step was to find a room which could afford my clients and me a reasonable degree of privacy. This was not easy: the only space available at the time was a small room next to the toilets, in some bleak anonymous corridor. It perhaps concretely expressed the view of some of the medical staff that counselling was about dealing with the unwanted by-products of their work. However, as the service became more firmly established I was later offered a more suitable space within the unit: perhaps a concrete expression of the improved status of counselling in the scheme of things?

The next step was to publicise the new service. I visited the staff in the various different areas of the unit, encouraging them to mention my service to their patients. I put up posters and advertised in the patients' magazine. The fact that I was personally well known to my nursing and medical colleagues allowed them to set aside to some degree their mistrust of counselling. The culture in so many medical services is based on the expectation that patients should meet their illnesses with stoicism, be grateful that they can receive the benefits of modern technical medicine, and above all, not to make a fuss. This very traditional British 'stiff upper lip' approach may work better for the staff who have to inflict some very unpleasant procedures on their patients, but to many cultures it is quite alien and it has never worked for a sizeable minority of the British when they become ill. The suspicion is that counselling somehow permits patients to become aware of how upset they are, which is a bad thing. It took time to demonstrate that counselling can also enable patients to manage their technical care more effectively and to live their lives more confidently. Any member of the medical and nursing team could make referrals if they were concerned about a patient's failure to cope with their illness, or patients could refer themselves.

Relationships with the hospital team: boundaries

At first it was hard for the patients and staff to adapt to a structured appointments system. Often treatment or medical appointments would change, preventing the client from attending a counselling session and creating obstacles to providing an efficient service. On some occasions it was difficult to establish whether lateness on the part of a client was due to an issue within the counselling process, such as avoidance, or to changes in treatment schedules. The patients in all other areas had to fit in to suit the availability of the machinery and their schedules would repeatedly be changed. One of the ways that they could empower themselves during the counselling would be to take some control over the timing of their attendance. I was forced to be more flexible with appointments and during meetings I encouraged staff to inform me of any changes and to be aware of the importance of keeping appointments.

Maintaining boundaries as a counsellor within a medical setting is problematic. It was not uncommon for staff to enter the room during a counselling session, and it took some time to help them understand the impact this had on the working alliance. Sometimes clients would be too ill to attend a session so I would visit them on the ward. This had the effect of making the therapeutic alliance less safe and inhibited the work; however, it did mean that some contact could be made. An example of this occurred whilst I was seeing a man on the ward who was dying. I was interrupted by the new registrar who insisted he had to carry out a minor medical procedure immediately. I explained that I would be finishing this session in half an hour and I would let him know when the patient was free. He insisted several times, then eventually left. The patient was still able to use the session, but it was more difficult for him.

The NHS as a training organisation inevitably has a very high turnover of junior staff of all professions so an important part of establishing the counselling service has been the ongoing education of new recruits to the renal unit. The service is not yet sufficiently embedded in the culture of the unit that I can expect medical and nursing colleagues to remember to warn their juniors about the particular needs of counsellors and the importance of respecting boundaries.

Further developments

All referrals were then offered an assessment appointment with me. This was quite simply to establish the nature of the problem and whether I was the best person to deal with it. Following assessment I can offer my clients up to eight sessions and then we review progress. In the early days all kinds of social and housing problems were referred to me, many of which required the input of a social worker. It also quickly became clear that several sessions might be taken up with explaining aspects of the treatment and offering guidance about external sources of information and support. Sometimes I needed to refer the client on for more formal psychiatric attention. I was fortunate to have a consultant psychotherapist on the team who provided one session a week for psychiatric input in terms of assessment and supervision.

The introduction of this new counselling service quickly uncovered other deficiencies in the psychosocial care of our patients. This led to the establishment of a dedicated social worker who could offer practical help and advice in relation to benefits, housing and other aspects of social care. Another development, which arose out of my early experience, was the need for straightforward education of patients and their families about renal failure and its treatment. This led to the establishment of two full-time nurses to work in the Low Clearance Clinic. This is a clinic for patients with chronic progressive renal impairment who were approaching end-stage renal failure. The nurses spend time with the patient and his or her family explaining the information they have been given and exploring the implications of chronic illness, haemodialysis and transplantation.

This has the effect of decreasing anxiety and uncertainty, allowing some anticipatory grieving and instilling hope for the future. Kelly-Powell (1997) has emphasised the value of generating an optimistic outlook which fosters confidence in the service when patients are facing life-long treatment for a potentially fatal disorder. This work is not strictly counselling and the expansion of nursing provision to the clinic freed me to concentrate on the counselling provision. The nurses were able to refer to me those patients who were unable to come to terms with their probable future, or were in other ways unable to cope with their illness.

With the growth of the service came the need for administrative support to deal with enquiries, book appointments and audit our activity. A full-time secretary was employed.

During the time the counselling service has been in existence, the renal unit has grown beyond recognition. There has been a five-fold increase in the number of patients under its care: there are 150–180 people on haemodialysis, 100 on continuous ambulatory peritoneal dialysis and between twenty and thirty kidney transplants are performed every year. A separate transplant clinic monitors about 200 post-transplant patients for any complications, such as rejection of the graft. A nurse is now attached to this clinic, again in an educational role, but able to identify patients who may benefit from a counselling intervention.

In this way a team of five people has grown from the original six-month pilot project. I lead and supervise the team which meets weekly for mutual support, peer supervision and review.

Transplant surgery

There is no doubt that renal transplantation greatly improves the quality of life of patients in chronic end-stage renal failure (Brown 1992). In

Norway, 80–85 percent of clients in kidney failure receive a transplant within 6–9 months (Jakobson 1995). However, in the UK the wait can be more than two years. For those people who have little hope of a cadaver transplant (that is, an organ transplant from a person who before his or her death expressed a wish to donate) living-related or non-related kidney donation is an option. This is a growth area in transplant surgery but it also introduces a whole new dimension to the task of the counselling service, as the impact of family dynamics cannot be ignored.

Renal doctors are under pressure to increase transplantation rates as more patients are joining the transplant programme than are leaving it. The total number of people in the UK waiting for renal transplantation at the end of August 1999 was 4,759, a 3 per cent increase on 1998 (National Transplant Database, UK Transplant Support Service Authority). There is a danger that doctors will 'sell' transplantation and living-related donation too enthusiastically, failing to warn patients and donors alike of some of the emotional stresses. To patients on long-term dialysis, the idea can grow that transplantation will be the miracle that will transform their lives. For many people it is the hope that sustains their capacity to persevere with the exacting regime of dialysis. They may be unprepared for the 'down side' of life with a new kidney. For others who are able to adapt to the regime, perhaps having successfully managed dialysis from within the role of such a person for many years, a transplant may prove a major emotional challenge. Littlefield (1992) stated that 'reintegration within both the family and the larger social network may be complicated and there is a great need for support'.

Living kidney donors are exposed to the risk of a major operation and a mortality rate of 0.03–0.06 per cent has been reported in the literature. Other potential risks include pulmonary embolism, haemorrhage and chest infections. Adverse psychological responses in both the donor and recipient populations have been recorded. This has been our experience too. For this reason we have developed a protocol for the psychological preparation of potential living related donors.

Any patient who wishes to be considered for a kidney transplant is first of all offered an appointment with our transplant co-ordinator. She discusses what is involved in general with the patient and if he or she wishes to proceed, the necessary medical investigations are arranged. If the test results are satisfactory, at the point of being accepted on to the programme the patient is asked if he or she is willing for us to contact any relative who may be a suitable live donor.

Counselling within the family

We contact possible related donors and invite them to a group information session in which kidney failure and kidney transplantation, including the benefits of live-related over cadaver donor transplants, are presented. This meeting also allows us to make a preliminary assessment of the family interactions. I then offer each family member, including the potential recipient of the transplant, four sessions of individual counselling. If English is not the family's first language the sessions are conducted with an independent interpreter who is not connected to the family.

Any family member who wishes to be considered as a potential donor must then undergo medical tests and tissue typing. If theirs is a good match and no medical complications are identified, I meet both potential donor and recipient in order to clarify their motivation and feelings about the proposed procedure.

There are many controversial issues involved with living-related transplantation and not everyone is persuaded that it is ethical. In a survey of nurses Kiberd and Kiberd (1992) identified 38 per cent who had difficulty accepting live-related transplantation. Some health professionals believe it is wrong to subject a healthy person to unnecessary surgery. Others believe we have no right to obstruct an altruistic act. Doctors may become partisan, favouring the needs of 'their' renal patient over those of a potential donor and his or her family. Pressure to donate is a reality, whether overt or covert, internal or external. Research carried out at Helsinki University showed that the risk of trauma to the donor increases when the recipient is a sibling, whereas the donation of a kidney to one's own child is usually easier to endure emotionally. However, a transplant between siblings is more likely to be successful. A clear conflict exists in this regard between medical and psychological interests.

The potential donor may discover a hitherto unexpected illness which prevents them saving the life of a loved one. Sometimes the decisions to consider donations are reached in isolation from other important family members, resulting in friction if the recipient is believed to be valued above a spouse or other dependent relatives. Equally the decision not to donate can lead to guilt or shame.

If the family dynamics are inadequately explored it is not unusual for a kidney transplant to be eventually rejected though non-compliance with post-operative drug regimes. In some cases the recipient of a kidney may harbour aggressive feelings towards the relative who has donated the organ. As a result, these feelings may be expressed by destroying the part inside themselves that represents that person, ending in the loss of a functioning transplant.

On one occasion I was counselling a mother who wished to donate a kidney to her daughter. The relationship between the two had been so volatile that the daughter was reluctant to accept the donation but could not express this to her mother. Overwhelming feelings of guilt and helplessness had driven the mother to offer her kidney as a resolution. However, the daughter was unable to resolve feelings of anger towards her mother and it was clear that, in this instance, living-related transplantation would put a further burden on an already strained relationship. It was therefore considered inappropriate to continue with the transplant, even though from a medical point of view the mother was an ideal donor. Both daughter and mother needed separate counselling to come to terms with both the decision and the issues surrounding chronic illness. This often creates a dynamic tension between the counsellor and the medical team as a power play is enacted.

Post-operative interventions

After a living-related transplant the recipient of the kidney may experience episodes of high anxiety and bouts of depression. Some clients pin all their hopes on a kidney transplant, believing it will solve all their problems. However, after the operation, they realise that the transplant has simply provided them with a different set of anxieties (Brown 1992).

I have found that during the first year following transplantation many transplanted clients experience depression and feelings of isolation. Other dialysis patients are often envious of a successful transplant and the client no longer feels part of the routine dialysis life. Staff may view a transplant as a successful outcome and are less prepared to be sympathetic to a transplanted client who is struggling with depression.

John, who was nine months post-transplant, was unable to sleep. He was also becoming obsessed with his fluid intake and urine output, constantly checking to see if they balanced, and fearing that his kidney was failing. After a clinic appointment he would wait by the telephone for the hospital to ring with his blood results, unable to leave the house. It took a long time for him to accept that the kidney was functioning and that he could start to build a new life for himself. He also struggled with feelings of gloom and felt burdened by the staff's expectation that he should be happier.

A kind of morality can creep into the staff–patient dynamics around a transplant in which the expectation is that the patient should do well out of gratitude to the staff and the donor, whether dead or alive. Depression, anxiety, crises of identity, poor compliance may then be judged adversely as evidence of ingratitude, leading to a degree of alienation between the patient and the staff.

I have also had clients referred whose kidney transplant has been rejected due to a reluctance to follow medical advice; that is, failing to take the drugs that are necessary to prevent the body rejecting the transplant. Often, medical staff are concerned about the appropriateness of offering these clients another opportunity especially as there is a shortage of organs for transplantation. In research carried out in the US into pre-transplant non-compliance and post-transplant outcomes, it was clear that there was a percentage of patients who persisted in non-compliant behaviour after receiving a second transplant. Following this research, recommendations were made that staff develop strategies to facilitate compliance in patients prior to transplantation, and it was found that it was possible to change the habits of patients who had shown episodes of non-compliance. Within my own group of clients, often the reason for non-compliance is unexpressed anger. This can be due to negative feelings about chronic illness, family relationships or job loss. Some clients are able to understand their behaviour when the depth of their anger is explored. This understanding often enables a client to approach transplantation positively.

Supervision

There is a marked increase at the moment in the demand for supervision within organisations such as the health service. Clinical supervision revolves around clinical professional issues and is often hierarchical, whereas counselling supervision is non-hierarchical. The most important part of supervision lies within the relationship itself. I see it as a restorative space, a play space where curiosity can allow us to explore alternative perspectives.

It was important to find a supervisor who had an understanding of hospital dynamics and who could support my work within a medical setting. It is important to have supervision outside of the organisation so that the context and culture of the work can be explored without contamination. The unit management agreed to make funding available for weekly supervision. Supervision helped greatly with the transition from the role of nurse to that of counsellor, as it was difficult at first not to be drawn back into the helping role. During the early stages, I was still seen by the staff as a nurse who could help out at busy times on the ward. I also found it difficult to give up the job that I could do confidently for a role in which I felt unsure and isolated. Gradually, over a period of time, the staff became more accepting of my role as counsellor as I became certain of my own boundaries.

Making the transition from nursing to counselling created difficulties in adapting from a nurturing role to one that required more detachment and objectivity. I initially experienced difficulties that we explored through the supervisory process. One hurdle was working as a counsellor in the same unit in which I had been a nurse. The staff were used to responding to me as a nurse and had difficulty relating to my role change. However, I find that my nursing knowledge is invaluable, in that I understand the medical treatments and conditions involved. As a result, the client can concentrate on looking at his or her feelings rather than explaining medical details. In addition, as a counsellor with renal knowledge, I am aware of times when clients may need to be encouraged to discuss symptoms with their doctor.

Steven was a 35-year-old man who referred himself for counselling. I arranged an assessment session which allowed Steven and me to explore what counselling could offer, and whether this was something he felt would be useful to him. I work from an integrative approach with a strong psychodynamic background. We needed to explore the issue of confidentiality because this is a concern for some clients within the unit. The reason for this is that the medical model in this unit believes that all information regarding clients is shared freely, and clients can feel unsafe coming to counselling. Steven needed to know that I provided a safe place for him to be in and that I discussed our work only with my supervisor, who was based outside the hospital setting. He said that he would like to work for eight sessions on a weekly basis exploring the frustration and anger that he had been experiencing recently.

Steven comes from a family where he is an only child; he now lives on his own. He described how three months ago within a week of seeing his doctor he had been diagnosed as having renal failure and found himself on dialysis. Initially he felt he had adapted well to his change in circumstances; he had read everything on the subject of renal failure and had returned to work, which was in advertising. However, he had recently been experiencing feeling low; this was also expressed when he described how he would exceed his fluid allowance, which he had previously been able to keep to, and this was affecting his health on dialysis.

Although these were medical issues, it was important to explore the anxieties that were driving the change in his behaviour. I felt that the presenting problem was that Steven believed he had lost his purpose in life, that there seemed no future for him and he had a sense of loss of control in his life.

Drinking more than he should allowed him both to test the boundaries and to take some of the control that he felt the staff had taken away from him. This had set up a conflict that allowed him to express his anger, which when explored was really about the loss of his health. The anger towards the staff was also an expression of both the frustrations that they could not make him better, and his inability to find something to blame for his illness. Steven felt that he could not cope with the responsibility of his condition and look after himself. He projected these feelings on to the staff, who were already dealing with the feelings of helplessness that are common when working with clients with a chronic illness.

The excessive drinking episodes became worse before they improved; there was even a counselling session during which he became quite breathless due to the fluid overload. That particular session seemed to be a turning point and had an effect on his approach. He had found it hard as a child to talk about feelings and felt very isolated: it sounds as if his feelings were often projected on to his mother, who he described as controlling, which had also been his experience of the staff on the unit. By clarifying his feelings and having the space to explore them, he was able to make connections with the past and present and he appeared less overwhelmed by his feelings and was able to look at his approach to his life.

We spent several sessions exploring endings, as a good ending would give Steven the opportunity to be more open and trusting of others rather than retreating and becoming defensive, which had been his coping mechanism in the past. Steven found these sessions useful in that he felt less anxious and overwhelmed by his feelings and able to look at future plans.

I need to be very clear about endings because another unusual feature about my work is that it is not uncommon for me to see the same client two or three years later about a different set of worries.

Issues of confidentiality the containment of anxiety and compliance

When setting up the counselling practice, confidentiality was a major concern for both the clients and the medical staff. It took time for clients to feel safe and accept that the counselling session was only discussed with my supervisor. This fear was partly because the renal unit functioned on the basis that client information is free for the staff to share and discuss. This is different to the basic philosophy of counselling regarding confidentiality, and it was some time before the clients entirely trusted me. The medical team saw me as withholding information from them, and this was perceived by some of the staff as quite threatening.

There were also some who were quite anxious and thought that the client might be discussing them; this situation had to be dealt with carefully. However, after discussion, it was agreed that if the client was referred by the medical team, I would simply record in the medical notes that I had seen the client and would keep detailed notes for my own records. In mental health teams it is possible to maintain confidentiality within the team. The medical model has a different ethos of free exchange and pooling of information, where confidentiality is seen as potentially dangerous.

There are many aspects to the role of a counsellor on a renal unit. On many occasions, I have become aware, mainly following observation of the behaviour and interactions of staff members, of my role being used to diffuse anxiety. Part of my work is to be able to provide clear boundaries and to stay within them, thus containing high levels of anxiety. There are often strong projections of unmanageable feelings of loss and helplessness from the staff within the unit and I can very easily find myself changing my practice. Supervision has been vital in enabling me to become aware of this process and in understanding the reasons behind it. I am therefore more able to help the staff by staying within my normal practice not stepping outside the established boundaries.

It is interesting that the hospital in which the renal unit is situated has undergone major structural change, in particular changes in management structure, and this may account for the high levels of anxiety. Without supervision, a counsellor can become caught up in these anxieties and find it difficult to remain outside them. Supervision has been vital in giving me a balanced view of certain behaviours. It has also helped me to respond appropriately rather than becoming drawn into heightened anxiety. One indication of the high level of anxiety is an increase in inappropriate referrals that have been considered as urgent. Whilst writing this chapter it has been brought to my attention that within my counselling role I have often been involved in other areas in the unit. This has led me to wonder whether it is my nursing background that has drawn me to change things that I believed could be improved. Another way of looking at this is that the nature of working with clients with chronic illness is so painful at times that I have needed to be able to have some part of my work which was more manageable.

Another area which causes an increase in anxiety levels is when a client on the renal unit makes the decision to discontinue his or her dialysis treatment. In reality, this distressing but often appropriate decision means that the patient will die without the support of dialysis. The staff respond to this type of decision in different ways. I am always asked to see the patient but often the reason for the referral is the hope that counselling may help to change the client's mind. I believe that many staff feel that I have failed if I do not achieve this. I have to be aware of projections from the staff that they wish me to rescue the client, and these overwhelming projections can tap into my own emotions.

A decision to discontinue treatment may lead to painful feelings of failure amongst staff and the sense that the client has rejected their care. Once again, supervision has helped me to understand the pressures involved in this particular aspect of counselling, and this has enabled me to remain present and focused during the session. Whatever decision is made by the client, I am faced with a dilemma. If the client chooses to continue treatment, I am seen as a hero; if not, the sense of failure experienced by the staff is projected onto me, resulting in a personal sense of isolation. The notion that counselling can change a client's mind affects future practice, and there is still a feeling of failure attached to the voluntary decision of a patient to die in some cases.

Evaluation of the service

The service has now been in operation for seven years and has been through a series of changes. Counselling within any large organisation is always challenging, as the counsellor needs to absorb the needs and objectives of that organisation as well as create their own. The organisation inevitably has an impact on the way the counsellor works. One of the main hurdles remains the need to educate staff about the counselling process every few months due to the rapid staff turnover.

Establishing boundaries for counselling practice and ensuring that appointments are kept are ongoing problems. In a private counselling practice these issues may not pose such a problem but in a hospital setting it demands a constant effort. In supervision the time is equally divided between the organisational culture and how it impacts on the counselling service and the client work itself. Working as a member of a team within a specialist unit has distinct advantages for the counselling process. Access to clients, even when critically ill, has always been easy. For the client, counselling is available at any stage of illness or well-being.

In the early days I found myself becoming involved in the organisational politics but more recently I have learnt to become more distant. This has allowed for a more focused approach to clients. At the same time I recognise the need to maintain a high profile within the unit in order to protect the counselling service, especially as areas increasingly have to fight to maintain resources.

The circle was recently completed when the team that had been developed was disbanded without consultation with the staff concerned. The work of the team was divided up and partitioned into separate areas. It is not known whether the team was seen as too powerful within the unit or whether it had become too visual a reminder of medical failures. The counsellor has relinquished her role as team leader and returned to the role of counsellor. It demonstrates the difficulties counsellors may experience if their work starts to impact on the functioning of the medical model, who may feel that the psychological aspects warrant less consideration than the physical aspects. When counsellors become proactive rather than reactive and encourage clients to become empowered, a dynamic tension between the physical and the psychological becomes enacted.

References

Brown, J.H. (1992) *Clinical Management of Renal Transplantation: Rehabilitation after Renal Failure*, Dordrecht: Kluwer Academic.

Jakobson, A. (1995) 'Live Renal Donation: a Way Forward?', in R.W.G. Johnson (ed.) *Transplantation '95. The outlook for transplantation towards 2000*. (Series No. 211, pp. 15–20), London: Royal Society of Medicine Press.

Kelly-Powell, M.L. (1997) 'Personalising Choices: Patients' Experiences with Making Treatment Decisions', *Research in Nursing and Health* **20**: 219–27.

Kiberd, M.C. and Kiberd, B.A. (1992) 'Nursing Attitude Towards Organ Donation Procurement and Transplantation, Kingston, Ontario, Canada', *Heart and Lung* **21**: (2): 106–111.

Littlefield, C. (1992) *Psychiatric Aspects of Organ Transplantation*, Oxford: Oxford Medical Publications.

Rosser, R.M. (1982) *Personal Meanings: Life with Artificial Organs. Renal Dialysis and Transplantation*, London: John Wiley.

Chapter 5

The development of a counselling service in a rehabilitation centre

Angela Taylor

Introduction

The role of counsellor in rehabilitation services across the UK is still taking shape. Although medical rehabilitation counsellors are growing in numbers, our work practices vary a great deal from centre to centre. We have a common bond, however, in creating and maintaining a space for emotional and psychological issues to be considered within a medical model based environment.

This chapter begins by describing the clinical setting of the King's College Hospital Rehabilitation Centre where the author works as a counsellor alongside other health professionals. I offer some background information about how the service was established and the rationale behind how it has evolved. The theme of the chapter is that rehabilitation work is difficult and stressful for all health professionals and that a variety of defences are used by individuals to cope with their responses to this work. I examine the culture in which our work takes place and consider how it might be possible to keep emotional issues on the agenda. This is crucial if patients are going to feel heard and contained by us as health workers. This process needs to provide staff with support and validation, in order that individuals do not become overwhelmed by emotional material and face 'burn-out'.

There is a broader look at the culture of the rehabilitation centre, which I describe as task-orientated (making and fixing things). This I feel is often reverted to as a natural defence for some staff. I go on to consider the differences in practice between the counsellor and other medical professionals, looking in particular at boundary issues. I also explore some of the emotional themes in this area of work; the most significant of these I believe to be loss. I draw the chapter to a close with a case study to illustrate some of the therapeutic issues encountered in my work with this client group and how complex dynamics between myself and other staff members can be created by patients' material.

There have been considerable developments in the team approach to patients' psychological health. However, we all need to remain open to monitoring our abilities and supporting each other as we support this challenging client group.

The rehabilitation centre: placing the counsellor in context

There are thirty-three rehabilitation centres in the UK providing outpatient rehabilitation services to people with a range of disabilities. At the time of writing, only fourteen of these have a counsellor as part of the multi-disciplinary team. I am the counsellor at King's healthcare rehabilitation centre in south-east London. The centre is headed by a consultant in rehabilitation medicine and includes prosthetists, orthotists, physiotherapists, an occupational therapist, a chiropodist, wheelchair therapists, rehabilitation engineers, management and administrative staff. The client group at such a centre comprises patients who have had an amputation or who have congenital limb deficiency, and patients using the other specialist services available. The role of counsellor was initially created exclusively for amputee patients. However, the extension of the specialist counsellor role at the King's rehabilitation centre has resulted in referrals from other client groups, for example from neuro-rehabilitation and general rehabilitation. The centre provides services to a population of 1.8 million people. This population has a considerable multicultural mix and a high level of lower socio-economic groups. The centre is very busy, with around eighty patients attending each day. It is not unusual for prosthetists and physiotherapists to be responsible for several patients at one time. Many of these patients are in poor general health and are severely limited in mobility and function.

Appointment of the counsellor

When I joined the centre in April 1996 there had been no counselling provision for about a year. Prior to that a medical member of staff was using counselling skills to support patients identified as having emotional difficulties related to their disability. The management had to decide how a counselling service could be created to meet the emotional and psychological needs of patients. After much thought and discussion with external advisers, a decision was made to appoint a qualified counsellor for two days a week. In March 1997 this increased to three days, and in January 1998 to four days a week because of the increasing number of referrals. In November 1999 a second counsellor was appointed for an additional two days a week.

The management requested that the new post-holder should receive counselling referrals and also set up a team of patient volunteers to meet and support new amputee patients. This can be very useful in order to provide practical information and offer understanding from a position of experience to new patients. However, from the outset I expressed concern about possible difficulties and complications involved in this task.

From my experience in the voluntary sector I felt that a group of volunteers would have to be screened very carefully to ensure that they had come to some level of acceptance of their situation in a healthy way and were not using the idea of 'helping others' to work through their own feelings. I was also aware of the training and supervision that would be required in order to support and monitor the work the volunteers were engaged in. After a short time I realised that I did not have the time available to address all these difficulties adequately and also continue to accept a growing number of referrals. What has evolved quite naturally as an alternative seems to work well. Following discussions with other medical staff, I now have a shortlist of patients that I believe possess appropriate skills and an adequate level of self-awareness to meet new patients. I can call on these individuals when required. I have discussions with them before and after contact with a new amputee so that they can explore any issues that present themselves. As a result of these considerations, I work predominantly with outpatients based at the rehabilitation centre. I also have some input at several local hospitals where appropriate.

The patient profile

People have an amputation for many different reasons. These include: peripheral vascular disease; diabetic complications leading to necrosis of the lower limbs; different forms of cancer; meningococcal septicaemia; and traumatic injuries ranging from road traffic accidents to gunshot wounds. There are also a small number of patients who have had a limb amputated following suicide attempts.

In my view the context and reason for the amputation is extremely relevant to the emotional reaction the patient may experience, and could therefore affect what might be asked of the professional working with him or her, both on an emotional and practical level. Working in the current NHS environment, it is likely that the demands of the patient will be greater than the support that staff are able to provide, due to the pressures of time and limited resources. Staff are rarely able to see patients on their own and may be dealing with several patients in a fitting room or a gym, and private conversations are a luxury not often available.

The National Health Service: a changing environment?

The above scenario is familiar in the modern-day health service. Staff are expected to perform their tasks as quickly and as efficiently as possible. Maximum clinical activity and reduction of waiting lists become the drive for performance. This pressure is exacerbated by the current competitive nature of healthcare provision, as different NHS trusts compete for contracts from local health authorities. As well as providing care for patients, staff must also make time available to carry out clinical audits of their work to provide evidence of their efficiency. It is of course necessary to monitor healthcare services; however, time to do this is difficult to find amongst the swift flow of patients created by the competitive ethos in the health service today.

It could be argued that the health service has represented a maternal and nurturing presence within our society, a 'good object 'that we could depend on and have high expectations of. People had faith in healthcare as if it were a religion. However, its role is changing to adapt to ever-growing populations and financial considerations. It could be seen as adopting more masculine characteristics. For example, science and technology now play a key part in caring for people. Business terminology and marketing approaches are now commonplace within the hospital infrastructure. The general public and staff working in the healthcare system have their faith tested by the consequences of these changes.

The modern-day health service demands more and more from staff. Indeed, MacKegney (1989) describes medical education as 'a neglectful and abusive family system'. She identifies qualifying features for this definition as 'unrealistic expectations, denial, indirect communication patterns, rigidity and isolation'. The hospital can be a chaotic and hostile place to be in. Murphy (1992) observes that: 'Technology has overwhelmed medicine and science has suffocated the art of healing, invading the space where healing is supposed to take place.'

Despite the fact that the rehabilitation centre is an outpatient unit, it still has the institutional atmosphere of a hospital. Staff work amongst machinery and technology and attempt the difficult task of making patients feel as if they are in a relaxed and friendly environment. This is particularly challenging for the prosthetists, whilst carrying out their task of making the artificial limbs. During assessment for a new prosthesis, the patient is required to stand up in his/her underwear and have the residual limb covered in cling film and then in a plaster cast, in order to achieve a perfect fit. Some prosthetists will explain clearly what is happening whilst others may not. Some patients may experience this as persecutory, some may feel humiliated and vulnerable in this situation, and it is the prosthetist's responsibility to try and make the patient feel more comfortable. In order to do this there must be some acknowledgement that the process may make a patient feel this way in the first place, but this may not be possible.

Working within a caring profession can be extremely stressful and anxiety-provoking and it is inevitable that staff will experience an unconscious wish to avoid these feelings. A variety of defences come into play to cope with a complex range of reactions. Menzies Lyth (1988) in her study of the nursing service in a general hospital revealed that the work practices in place often act as a protection against the difficult feelings that can be stirred up for staff.

The counsellor's presence and institutional defences

I should like to look at how the rehabilitation team has responded to having a counsellor in its midst. My arrival has to some extent disrupted the defence mechanisms put in place to cope with the anxiety and distress that working with people with illness and disability creates. In other ways it has created new ones.

It has taken some time for me to be accepted as a part of the multi-disciplinary team. When I arrived I felt it was unclear to some staff how I would fit into the work group that had been functioning for sometime without a counsellor. For people who did not have any experience of counselling in any way, it felt as though my presence was a bit of a mystery. Who was I? What was I doing there? I was treated warily at first and immediately realised that I would need to work to convince staff that I was approachable. Some staff ignored me and did not quite know how to relate to me. McKenzie (1996) describes a similar process at the GP practice where she works, suggesting that she has a range of negative feelings from staff projected onto her; she says: 'I am ignored, not spoken to as I walk past, and I feel invisible.'

I am also aware that the counsellor in a team can be a target for projections, and this can create a split between the counsellor and the rest of the group. I have worked hard to understand this splitting process, which is in some ways inevitable but needs to be acknowledged so that the team can remain functional. Noonan (1983) talks about the possibilities of confusion arising in organisations: 'For counsellors, most difficulties arise because the nature of their work is poorly understood by others, and it is often felt to be at variance with the objectives of others.'

I have to keep communication lines open with all staff. When new members of staff come on board, I like to introduce myself and explain my role in order to diffuse any mystery. I like to know that I have engaged with the individual and that there has been an understanding of my task within the service which we give to patients using the centre.

My presence immediately puts emotional and psychological factors on to the workplace agenda for all staff. In expecting other members of the multidisciplinary team to make appropriate referrals to me, I am requesting that they start to think about patients as real people with families and lives, rather than depersonalising individuals with medical terminology, for example, 'the diabetic lady with a right trans-tibial'. I am suggesting that they attempt to notice and take in the emotional responses of patients. Apart from the fact that there may be limited time to do this, staff members will have their own feelings to cope with that inevitably emerge whilst listening to the patient. Some members of staff have talked about feeling helpless, upset and at times overwhelmed with grief and sadness at what patients tell them about their lives.

As well as providing a service for patients, the role of counsellor in a multidisciplinary team requires the facilitation and containment of such feelings evoked in staff, so that patients' difficulties can then be heard. However, it is important not to dismantle defences completely to the extent that the medical team cannot function. Moylan (1994) suggests that 'staff need to develop defences in order to cope. Some defences are necessary and can serve development, creativity and growth'.

This involves paying attention to team dynamics as we go about our work. It means encouraging and supporting staff when they need to acknowledge and discuss their struggles about particular patients whilst holding in mind the consequences of searching their internal world of feelings. Some members of staff have welcomed the opportunity to talk to me about their reactions to patients and have spoken of their relief at being able to acknowledge difficulties. One conversation may be enough to contain their anxieties and enable them to understand some of the issues that may be affecting their work with a patient. This leads to an ability to empathise with their patient much more. Where it has been possible to have constructive discussions with staff, I have consequently received unexpected feedback from patients who feel that their relationship with a prosthetist or physiotherapist has improved considerably, because they have felt heard and understood.

I have encountered some hesitancy in staff when it comes to making a counselling referral. For example, it is important that the patient agrees to the referral and so the medical professional working with the patient needs to discuss this with them. Some staff fear they will be accused of suggesting either that the patient can't cope or that the patient is 'mad'. They are also afraid that if they suggest a counselling referral they will unleash a range of powerful emotions from the patient that they will find hard to deal with. As a result of the expression of these anxieties about broaching the issue of counselling I have introduced some training and discussion workshops. These sessions have enabled staff to look at what lies behind their reluctance to suggest seeing a counsellor and to explore ways of listening to and talking with patients in a way that is manageable for staff and patients alike. A valuable part of these sessions has been to provide some time for staff to acknowledge to each other how emotionally draining their job can be. Members of staff seem extremely relieved to take the space to share their feelings in this way. They have been in need of some support in their struggles to cope with the day-to-day onslaught of sometimes hopeless situations.

Although some members of staff will allow themselves to feel their emotions, others may feel uncomfortable discussing the possibility that the work they are doing with a patient has an emotional component to it. They may be accustomed to having their defences in place at work. It is important to find this balance of allowing rather than forcing staff to consider some of these issues. Otherwise their instinct may be to minimise and deny the impact of the patient's condition both for themselves and the patient, and ultimately to deny that there is any need for a counsellor as part of their medical team.

Holding this position as counsellor can present complex difficulties. I often have the feeling that, in facilitating discussion in this way, there is always a part of me that remains outside the team. I am both a member of a system and yet an observer of it, attempting to remain objective; this can be isolating at times. This issue highlights the split that exists, which is represented in our different ways of working. It can lead to the staff regarding me stereotypically as 'too serious' or 'too soft'. This issue becomes relevant when a patient's rehabilitation programme is not going well. It may be that the staff have higher expectations than the patient's confidence levels will allow them to reach. Or perhaps a patient will become demoralised by his/her physical limitations and become depressed even though s/he has just been given a high-tech intelligent prosthesis. As counsellor I may have access to personal information that explains a patient's difficulties whereas a physiotherapist, for example, may feel quite frustrated by the apparent apathy of a patient. Therefore, we shall have quite different perceptions of the same person.

What are the defences keeping at bay?

For patients the most common reaction to the loss of a limb can be described as grief, comparable to that experienced after a close bereavement. This may include difficulty in accepting the amputation; anger; pining for the lost body part and the sense of being incomplete; guilt; and profound sadness. Parkes (1991) writes about this loss and concludes that 'the psychosocial transition from being an intact person to being an amputee is a painful and time consuming process which is, in many ways, similar to the transition from married person to widow or widower'. These responses to having an amputation can be very distressing to witness.

A person who has had an amputation displays a visible loss and mutilation of his/her body. Perhaps this makes the need to distance oneself even more urgent, for both staff and family members. I can still remember seeing my first 'stump' or residual limb on a ward round, and it was not the amputation wound that affected me but the space where the leg should have been. As the patient began to describe the phantom sensation of feeling that the limb was still intact, I began to feel uncomfortable and then nauseous as I stared at the vacant space. It could be argued that it represents an internal void in ourselves that needs to be initially denied and then filled. The wish to replenish this empty space may be felt more acutely by some staff than others, depending on their own experiences of both loss and absence.

It is noteworthy that as soon as a patient is physically healed a prosthesis will be fitted and made for a patient. The ideal scenario for medical staff would be for patients to learn to walk with their new prostheses before they have left hospital. This is of course the only way that patients can quickly regain some mobility and function. However, I have often wondered whether there is enough time for the patient to reflect on the loss of the limb and allow some of the feelings about the situation to be processed. The patient is often surrounded by both family and medical staff who are keen to see them standing upright, with the 'awful gap' where their leg or arm used to be filled with a replacement. It is in some ways analogous to the urgent wish to become pregnant again after the loss of a pregnancy, when perhaps it is better for parents to wait for a while so that the meaning of the loss can be considered (Bowlby 1991). In fact, I have noticed that there are similarities between work with amputees and previous work I have done with women who have experienced a loss of pregnancy. This is particularly relevant to pre-amputation counselling, where it is possible to consider the impact of the loss prior to surgery. In my opinion it is valuable for emotional exploration and information-giving to take place at this stage of both procedures (Walker 1990). It can mean that that the grieving process is less likely to become complicated and prolonged, as in termination of pregnancy, for example. However, in both cases, this is not always possible. There is often a feeling from medical personnel that if a traumatic procedure is to take place then it should go ahead as soon as possible.

Overall culture of the rehabilitation centre

I have observed that there is a problem-solving culture in place at the rehabilitation centre. The main tasks are to make and fix things in order to improve patients' function and mobility. For example, the orthotists will make special shoes and appliances; the prosthetists will create and repair artificial limbs; the rehabilitation therapists and engineers will make the most comfortable and appropriate wheelchair for a patient; physiotherapists will teach patients how to walk with their prostheses, and so on.

Most of the staff at the centre possess valuable technical and mechanical problem-solving skills, along with an expectation of functional success and positive outcome in sometimes quite hopeless circumstances. Sometimes patients may feel disappointed with their new prostheses or wheelchair, and may become upset or angry and non-compliant. This may be very frustrating for staff. It is sometimes the case that patients repeatedly return to the centre with complaints about their prosthesis. This may sometimes be an unconscious communication about their loss of a part of themselves, which no artificial limb can replace. Where it has been possible to refer these patients for counselling to speak about their loss, their appointments for prosthetic adjustments have decreased considerably. The staff members' ability to cope with emotions displayed by patients if results are disappointing will be influenced by the staff's own internal resources and external support levels.

Patients with a chronic illness can be dependent and regressed and may seek containment of difficult feelings from the medical team. I am referring to Bion's (1962) theory of containment, in which a baby (patient) seeks a container for confusing and overwhelming feelings that they are unable to bear or make sense of. The medical staff will be seen as potential containers in which the patient at an infantile level can get rid of these feelings. This can be extremely demanding for some staff, especially if they have not experienced adequate containment of difficult feelings themselves. Childhood experiences of staff may influence the level of distress that they can tolerate. This situation can awaken primitive feelings of helplessness in carers and staff, particularly if this process is not within their conscious awareness. Defences may then be mobilised to avoid these uncomfortable feelings and these will present themselves in different forms. I am probably not alone in hearing the hostile and critical judgements made by staff about the most needy of patients, who are sometimes quite unbearable to be with because their distress or anger feels so unmanageable. Such patients can project the most desperate and violent rageful feelings into staff. As counsellor I am invited to collude with defences to avoid these feelings. When I resist the collusion it often places me outside the team, working with a different approach to such difficult feelings: 'Staff groups will tend to avoid understanding or dealing with what is projected into them in this way, and deal with their unprocessed emotions by themselves relying on projective identification as a means of getting rid of what feels too painful' (Moylan 1994).

I have the opportunity through supervision to explore ways of staying with such difficult feelings and to help patients to understand and find meaning in them. Without the opportunity to reflect on the feelings evoked by such patients in a supportive environment the inevitable distancing and denial of such feelings will be the only way that staff may be able to continue working with them. It is possible that a team culture of denial will come into place. If staff feel that their management does not value them enough to provide support for the difficult work they do, then the result could be a feeling that the matriarchal container of the NHS as an employer has failed them. This may lead to stress levels becoming unbearable and sickness absence increasing, resulting in possible burn-out. These issues have resource implications; however, the long-term effects of this form of investment could bring more job satisfaction and therefore increase cost-effectiveness.

I can attempt to offer exploration of these issues on a small scale in the rehabilitation centre on an *ad hoc* basis. However, I am sometimes seen as the reason why patients are depressed or upset. I have sensed an implicit message that I would describe as: 'This patient was all right until you started work with them. What have you done to them? You have created this mess so you had better get rid of it.' Patients may get in touch with difficult feelings in counselling which may then become apparent to other staff. There can be resentment that you are seen to have forced those hidden painful feelings into the open. Again, Noonan (1983) identifies this problem:

> A counsellor on the premises does implicitly sanction the acknowledgement of problems, and those in difficulty will come forward making it appear that the counsellor has created the problems. The fault lies not in the counsellor but in primitive logic.

As I said above, I often feel I am working at odds with the general ethos of the team, which could be to think positively in the face of distress. In contrast I attempt to enable patients to face the darkness of illness and disability, to face the negative side of a situation, to understand its meaning, and this may be difficult for other staff to tolerate.

Differences in work practice

I am often aware of being in an enviable position, of being able to give one patient at a time my undivided attention. Hospital transport permitting, I am probably the only person in the centre who is able to stick to appointment times.

Working within a psychodynamic framework, the time boundaries of a counselling session and how a patient uses them are ways of noticing clues to unconscious communication. This setting presents frequent dilemmas and interesting scenarios for me to observe. If a patient is late for a first session I may be inclined to interpret some unconscious resistance to attend counselling. This may be true; however, it may be that the patient's experience of the NHS appointment system is that they are rarely seen on time. If there is no other reason for the patient's late arrival then they are usually on time for subsequent sessions.

Some members of staff are initially puzzled by my adherence to the timing of the therapeutic hour. However, where possible I discuss this issue with staff and they are usually interested in its significance for me and respect my work practices much more as a result. This issue is particularly pertinent if a patient has another appointment in the centre before seeing me. Most staff members now know that I prefer them not to bring a patient round to my room fifteen minutes before their appointment time, as I am then faced with the dilemma of whether to send the patient away or start the session early. At other times I have to demonstrate flexibility. For example, I may have to wait if a patient is due to start their counselling session with me but instead is sitting in the fitting room in their underwear with no prosthesis on, having been told that it will be ready in five minutes. This does mean that the patient's choice, whether conscious or unconscious, to be early or late for a session, is taken away from them. We are then both deprived of the opportunity to illuminate feelings about their attendance. Segal (1995) speaks about this kind of dilemma if, for example, a patient's transport fails to collect him/her: 'If a counsellor normally interprets failure of a client to arrive does this still apply?'

She also explores the issue of the counsellor's ground rules and how these may be tested by patients with disabilities. For instance, I have been invited to take on an advocacy role, which as counsellor I have resisted, whereas other members of staff have taken this on more readily.

The message of the work

As I have mentioned, the overwhelming emotional response from patients to their situation is some form of grief for the losses involved. Those include loss of self-esteem; loss of identity and status; loss of positive self-body image; loss of future possibilities. A patient's whole sense of self may feel as if it is falling apart.

A process of adjustment and acceptance is likely to take some time and this can be complicated by other psychological events that may be triggered off by a traumatic event such as an amputation or the onset of illness. The life of a patient may, as a context, have many other unresolved conflicts and traumas, which emerge in counselling. In my experience these cover a wide range of issues including war experiences, childhood abuse, displacement and separation issues, rape, sexual violence, and bereavement. It is not uncommon for these experiences to surface during counselling. It is then necessary to consider them and reflect on how they relate to the current situation. Past experiences will usually have some bearing on what coping resources are available to patients as they face their difficulties.

Case history

I wish to look at one patient's story in order to illustrate the significance of past events for the rehabilitation process, and how this influences her relationships with medical staff.

Referral

I met Anna on a routine ward round in hospital. She was 19 years old at that time and had been admitted to the accident and emergency unit with a meningitis diagnosis, which developed into meningococcal septicaemia. Following several weeks on an intensive care ward Anna was transferred to an open ward. The medical team made heroic attempts to save her legs, which were very badly infected. These attempts failed, and due to the blood poisoning she had both legs amputated below the knee.

After our initial meeting on the ward, I did not see Anna until almost nine months later, as she had declined the offer of counselling up to that point. After being at home for several months she began to deteriorate emotionally and life became extremely difficult for her to cope with. She self-referred after a meeting with the consultant at the centre, who identified her feelings of frustration and despair.

Assessment

During our first session we discussed what Anna might want from counselling. She had experience of a difficult family therapy assessment several years earlier. During this meeting she had not felt valued or heard. She had therefore declined the offer of counselling when it was offered in hospital because she was wary of opening herself up to someone again. However, during our first session she was able to speak about her feelings of despair and isolation. She acknowledged that she needed someone to help her make sense of what she was feeling.

Contract

We agreed to meet for six sessions, during which time we would explore the issues with which she was struggling. These issues included the breakdown of communication with her family, on whom she was so dependent in her new situation. She also spoke about her fears regarding her future. There was much uncertainty about how her life might take shape now. It became clear to me that these areas would require further exploration.

At the end of these six sessions Anna said that she had felt a sense of relief talking about herself, although it had been very painful. She acknowledged her fears about 'falling into the depths of despair' and yet she wanted to find a way through her difficult feelings. She expressed a wish to continue with counselling and we agreed to continue working together indefinitely.

Process and content

What followed during the next two years of counselling was a process of exploration into Anna's internal world. Her history became more and more relevant to understanding both her defence mechanisms during her illness and her expectations of herself and others in this crisis time.

Anna's childhood environment was described as chaotic and unpredictable. Her father had a severe mental illness, which predated her birth, and her mother spent much of her time caring for him, as well as trying to care for Anna and her two brothers. Anna experienced her childhood carers as being inconsistent and unreliable. She had felt afraid of her father's outbursts and found him both threatening and patronising. She felt that her mother's attempts to protect or understand her were ineffective. In fact, it appeared that Anna had become a support for her mother during her early years and into adolescence, rather than the other way around.

Anna had defended herself against her own feelings of anger and disappointment with a range of self-destructive patterns including alcohol misuse, damaging relationships and manic activity, blocking off awareness of her emotional needs because she did not know how to respond to them.

Her early experiences are relevant in terms of how she perceived the medical care she received, both in hospital and at the rehabilitation centre. Whilst in hospital she became extremely childlike and her regression was intensified by the constant presence of her mother, who came forward to care for Anna in a way that Anna had wanted for years. Anna was very frightened, wary of being hurt by medical procedures and concerned about not being cared for properly while she was in such a vulnerable state. She was quite an anxious patient, and some staff found this challenging.

Anna found being dependent on others in hospital difficult. She was keen to get walking with her artificial legs, and therefore regaining some level of mobility and strength was a high priority for her. It became clear after her discharge from hospital that she would not be able to return to life as it was before. The whole experience of contracting meningitis and the amputation of her legs had been so traumatic that she was unable to use her previous defences to cope with all her feelings. At this point she referred herself for counselling.

Anna's key relationships in the centre are with me, with her prosthetist and with the consultant. The potential for her to split us off into good or bad parent figures is enormous. It has been necessary therefore to keep open the lines of communication between all of us as Anna goes through her rehabilitation programme, so that we minimise the likelihood of getting caught up in this splitting process. This hopefully helps to make her feel more contained by the team.

We have all been aware as individuals of the projections put onto or into us at various times. My role has been quite complex, being both aware and part of these dynamics. I have seen my task as being to encourage Anna to become aware of her transferential feelings towards all of us, in order that she may gain insight into relationships in general and think about how she might gain most from relating to others.

For a short time Anna was in conflict with the centre consultant, and, I believe due to her transference response to him, experienced his care as being somewhat patronising and dismissive, as if he were speaking to a child. At the same time, the consultant, in a counter-transference response, felt Anna to be quite demanding and hostile, and was somewhat exasperated by her. This was a change in what was a very productive relationship. During the exploration of this relationship in her counselling sessions we were able to make the link between her expected responses from a 'father figure', that is, unpredictable and punitive reactions towards her, and her feelings towards the consultant. She began to be able to express some of her anger and disappointment about her childhood relationship with her father. It then became possible for Anna to think about the consultant in relation to her current needs as an adult, and to think about alternative ways of relating to him. In turn, freed from these particular projections, the doctor became aware of a change in her behaviour, in that he saw her as becoming more assertive and clear about her needs in the here and now, and could respond to her more readily as an adult.

Supervision

During this time I felt Anna's unconscious splitting between the consultant as a hostile paternal figure and myself as maternal object that she hoped would provide her with a reparative experience by defending her position. In supervision I began to experience my older male supervisor as unsupportive. I was holding Anna's experience of being criticised. It was through discussion of my feelings that we became aware of a parallel process occurring. This freed me to speak about what I felt to be Anna's plea to come up with solutions to her difficulties.

My supervisor helped me to understand the process and contain my own feelings of helplessness at this time. This gave me the courage to interpret her sense of abandonment and to discuss her expectations of me, rather than responding to her plea for a rescuer. Through supervision I had been able to untangle the projections and thus provide Anna with an understanding of her feelings. This process gave Anna the opportunity to explore her anger and disappointment about parent figures, whilst learning how to bear and contain these feelings for herself.

Working with unconscious processes

My work with Anna demonstrates the theoretical approach that underpins my work, in that I see my task as bringing unconscious anxieties and conflicts from the past into conscious awareness within the boundaried frame of the counselling relationship. I attempt to use transference and counter-transference responses to provide information about projections and splitting, therefore allowing clients to develop insight into their way of relating to the world, as they tell their stories. With this insight, clients hopefully become able to contain painful feelings, and begin to allow themselves exploration of ways of meeting their emotional needs. At present I am able to provide long-term contracts to allow this process to develop where appropriate.

Ending

Anna was forced by her change in circumstances to look at her life in a way she had never done before. She now believes that her illness has allowed her to break destructive patterns and challenge self-beliefs, so leading to the possibility for change. Although life presents Anna with many painful obstacles to self-growth, she has developed the courage to look at life squarely and honestly and has made some dramatic changes. She is more discriminating about her relationships with people and has the ability to acknowledge her needs and, where appropriate, can negotiate consideration of these.

My work with Anna is drawing to a close and we have spent some time working with what this means for her, in particular looking at issues of separation and loss. These issues are especially significant for Anna, as she has been faced with huge losses in the time that I have known her. She has also been able to explore her feelings of anger and sadness about what she has not been able to get from counselling. She has faced the reality that her pain cannot be taken away by a significant other, but that she can share her feelings with people she can trust. Anna has more appropriate expectations of people close to her, and is more able to ask for what she needs from them. Anna has selected a partner who is able to understand her needs and values and respects her. Her pattern of choosing partners that reinforced her negative self-beliefs began to change when she recognised her own self-worth and her right to be valued as an individual. Negotiating this relationship has presented many new painful challenges for Anna; however, she is currently making plans for marriage. It will be with great sadness that I conclude my work with Anna. I have learned a great deal from the experience and feel privileged to have been a witness to her continuing development.

Evaluation

It is now the practice of our counselling service to request that clients complete a clinical audit questionnaire when they finish their counselling work. This requirement is only a subjective indicator of their experience; however, it is a helpful provider of information about how our service is received by clients. In addition to this, where possible, it is my practice to see clients at a follow-up appointment three months after our work is finished. I have experienced great changes in Anna during my work with her and believe she has developed a strong sense of self during this time. I hope that Anna's ability to contain her feelings remains in place, to help her to cope with the changes that life brings. I shall be looking for evidence of continued exploration of issues with the insight she has gained in counselling. However, if at any time in the future Anna feels the need to explore new issues that present themselves then I would accept a referral for a new contract of work.

Conclusion

As a team our interactions are now more fluid, and collaborative work practices are a direct result of this. It is always essential for me to maintain confidentiality, of course, and this is now fully respected by the staff in the centre.

The work we are all involved with is challenging and difficult. In this chapter I have focused primarily on organisational dynamics that are in place to allow our work to continue. My role in the team continues to develop, particularly when staff changes take place. It is important that attending to team dynamics is an ongoing process.

As a counsellor working with this patient group, my own responses to the material I listen to also require ongoing monitoring and exploration. The feelings experienced at both a conscious and an unconscious level are powerful and overwhelming at times. The containment I enjoy from clinical supervision and supportive discussions with other counsellors in my field is invaluable to me.

Being a counsellor in any multidisciplinary team is isolating at times and I have often felt that there is a parallel process linking me with the patients I see. Namely, the sense of being 'different' to everyone else. I feel that a healthy awareness of my own limitations and difficulties helps me to identify areas that need ongoing exploration. This may come in the form of supervisory discussions, or training, or my own therapy. Segal (1995) talks about the stresses of working with people with disabilities and she concludes: 'the best recipe for overcoming many of the problems . . . is the experience of counselling them successfully. The initial difficulties, once overcome, become a source of strength and confidence for the counsellor.'

I feel it is important to acknowledge progress and success in our work as well as having a close eye on the darker areas that require illumination. It is an ongoing process for my colleagues and me in this area of work.

References

Bion, W.R. (1962) 'A Theory of Thinking', *International Journal of Psycho-analysis* **43**: 306–10.

Bowlby, J. (1991) *Attachment and Loss*, vol. 3, Harmondsworth, UK: Penguin.

MacKegney, C. (1989) 'Medical Education: a Neglectful and Abusive Family System', *Family Medicine Journal* **12**: 452–7.

MacKenzie, B. (1996) 'The Enemy Within', *Psychodynamic Counselling* 2 (3): 390–400.

Menzies Lyth, I. (1988) *Containing Anxiety in Institutions*, London: Free Association Books.

Moylan, D. (1994) 'The Dangers of Contagion', in A. Obholzer and V.Z. Roberts (eds), *The Unconscious at Work*, London: Routledge.

Murphy, N.M. (1992) *The Physician as Artist and Guide*, London: Haworth Press.

Noonan, E. (1983) *Counselling Young People*, London: Tavistock/Routledge.

Parkes, C.M. (1991) *Bereavement: Studies of Grief in Adult Life*, Harmondsworth, UK: Penguin.

Segal, J. (1995) 'The Stresses of Working with Clients with Disabilities', in W. Dryden (ed.), *The Stresses of Counselling in Action*, London: Sage.

Walker, M. (1990) *Women in Therapy and Counselling*, Buckingham, UK: Open University Press.

Chapter 6

Professional development through supervision and staff groups

Peter Thomas

Introduction

It is a truism that working with the mentally ill is stressful. Violence, unreason, self-harm, despair, perversion and negativity all challenge the mental health workers' faith in their capacity to help others. Add to this the social deprivation, interracial tension, the high levels of drug-related crime in the inner cities, and they may begin to feel they are alone in attempting to meet society's obligations to the mentally ill. Finally, organisational change, dismantling the discredited asylum model of care, replacing it with care in the community; the introduction of the NHS internal market, and more recently Trust mergers, endanger morale still further as nothing any longer seems dependable in a world dominated by 'efficiency savings' or service degradation.

There is a consensus that maintaining morale, well-being and motivation in staff is essential for commitment to high standards of practice (Borrill *et al.* 1996). There is also recognition that psychotherapeutically trained staff can provide supervision, training and support to 'front-line' mental health workers by providing models of understanding and managing mental distress (Parry 1996).

The staff support group, led by a suitably trained facilitator, has traditionally been a way of meeting the needs of front-line staff. This legacy of the therapeutic community movement has been a mixed blessing (Bolton and Roberts, in Obholzer and Roberts 1994), as it can be viewed by staff as a magical solution to the inherent difficulty of their work or it can be used defensively to prevent conflict resolution and change. Robertson and Davison (1997) suggest that, although a well-planned and well-led staff group can be helpful, in practice many of the groups they studied served only to increase anxiety or to reflect institutionalised defences of the organisation of which they were a part.

In this chapter I describe the development of a model of intervention with staff groups which attempts to foster conditions for constructive group work and to limit the regressive pull into the security of primitive institutionalised defences and rituals (Hirschhorn 1988).

Background

A review of NHS psychotherapy services in England (Parry 1996) stated that: 'The needs of staff working in mental health services should also be taken into account, specifically the use of psychotherapeutically trained staff in providing supervision, training and support to front line staff.' It went on to recommend that:

> The shortage of skilled practitioners suggests that their skills and knowledge are best deployed in providing support, training and consultancy to other mental health staff. It has been argued that this provides models of understanding and managing mental distress, informing and supporting staff who are under stress as a result of working with disturbed people.

In July 1996, as part of the NHS Workforce Initiative, a questionnaire feedback to the trust highlighted some interesting facts:

1   26.8 per cent were experiencing a relatively high level of stress.
2   The final predictor of job satisfaction is social support. This refers to the extent to which individuals receive practical and emotional support from their peers. Those who reported high levels of social support also reported higher levels of job satisfaction.

They recommended that 'any facilities for dealing with stress-related problems be promoted more widely throughout the Trust'.

In 1994 the Chief Executive of the Trust initiated a study to address the high levels of stress experienced by the staff on the in-patient wards. One of its recommendations was that 'the Trust draft its own policy on good staff support practices in the context of local need and existing resources'. As a result of this the Trust in 1996 comissioned the preparation of a staff support strategy. The report recommended the provision of a full staff support service. However, this was never implemented.

The Mental Health NHS Trust is in an area of high social and economic deprivation. It is ethnically complex and exhibits high psychiatric morbidity.

A tripartite model

This is a model I have developed, with supervisory help from Rance (1998a), over the last 10 years in my work with health workers in a wide variety of contexts (Thomas 1995). I shall first describe the three components and then outline my role and how it developed in the light of experience and reflection.

In the early days I worked with single grading groups at the request of the groups themselves (Thomas 1995). During the last 5 years I have moved towards developing professional development groups (PDGs) as described below.

I Professional development groups

A clear set of goals for these weekly staff meetings evolved to which prospective new members of the team were asked to agree as a condition of their joining the group:

* To develop effective multidisciplinary communication structures that might contribute to the effectiveness of team communication and lead to a greater understanding of and respect for the role of others. It was assumed that better communication would lead to improved patient care.

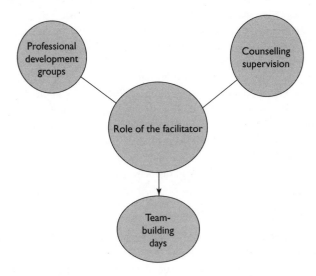

Figure 6.1 The tripartite model

- To give the staff a chance to develop reflective practice and encourage them to explore the effect of the work setting on their personal physical and psychological health. Reflection, as Johns (1993) says, 'involves a commitment to personal confrontation to expose the contradiction within experience between what the practitioner aims to achieve and the way they practice. It is the conflict caused by these contradictions that empowers the practitioner to take action.'
- To develop an awareness of how group culture can reflect the work or environmental culture, which in turn can reflect the culture of the organisation. By using the group as a diagnostic tool, rather than as a traditional supportive structure, the intention is that, with a correct diagnosis or, at least, a reasonable hypothesis, the members of the group are empowered to take steps to resolve issues outside the group in the daily life of the ward. They will hopefully become attuned to the interplay between their own personal valency for particular unconscious roles, and the institutional processes outside the group. The 'ambiguity view' put forward by Martin (1994) is that 'Culture is not the island of clarity within a jungle of meaninglessness – it is the jungle itself.'

These three main aims are not hidden; they are made clear to all new members of the group. The facilitator meets with every new staff member to talk about the purpose of the staff groups, the boundaries and their previous experiences of being a member of groups. The prospective group member can only attend the group when he/she has signed the bottom of the form agreeing to the group boundaries (see Appendix 6.1). The value of meeting with prospective members cannot be overstated. It gives both parties a chance for a human encounter prior to their joining the group. Any concerns about membership can be explored and the rationale for the groups explained. It also seems to have the effect of denying staff members immediate access to the groups whilst they await an individual meeting, which means they are left outside initially as their colleagues all disappear into the inner sanctum. This seems to create an urgency to join the group to find out what goes on.

2 Counselling supervision

The second part of the model looks at the supervisory structures that operate within the working environment. At present the author offers weekly one-to-one counselling supervision to the team leaders on the wards, but the long-term aim is to develop group supervisory structures.

There is a marked increase in the demand for clinical supervision within organisations such as the health service at the moment. The term clinical is used in an attempt to differentiate it from managerial supervision; however, both tend to be hierarchical and judgemental around management and professional issues. Counselling supervision is free from any lines of managerial or clinical authority or responsibilities and is strictly non-hierarchical.

The supervisor needs to create a facilitative, safe environment which is both bounded and confidential. Within this space lies room for a personal exploration of culture and context. I favour a high-challenge, high-support model, which incorporates exploring the normative, formative and restorative needs of the supervisee.

At first I wondered how it might impact on the group itself if I were to see a group member outside the group, and whether this would be interpreted as making that member special in some way. So far this issue has not arisen within the group. One contribution is that the facilitator is made aware of information that never appears in the PDGs themselves. This can help him function effectively, but one of the difficulties is trying to remember the context in which information has been received. Discussing this in my own supervision we felt that the best option was to refrain from offering anything new that had not originated from the group itself in the moment, except generalised comments.

This supervision is seen as a 'perk' of leadership. At times other group members have acted up for the team leaders, for example during maternity leave or prolonged absence, and they have been offered weekly supervision which was then withdrawn when they returned to their old roles. It is difficult to evaluate the impact this has had on the individuals concerned as they reverted back to their former status.

The additional information acquired through the supervisory process about individual group members must have some effect on the facilitator's position because any knowledge alters mental processes. I believe that the positive elements of this model outweigh any negative bias. If the group operates as a diagnostic tool and it is acknowledged that the issues diagnosed have to be worked on outside the group as well as inside, the supervision can be used to explore how this can be achieved. An example of this has been the development of team-building away-days and more effective supervision structures.

3 Team-building days

Team-building days (TBDs) are an important part of the model and are recommended to take place at six-monthly intervals. The groups, when being used effectively as a diagnostic tool, produce a large amount of material on which, due to the busyness of an acute mental health ward, there is little time to reflect. The TBDs give the teams a chance to spend time focusing on how to implement changes and to develop more effective communication structures.

One key contribution of TBDs is the presence of all the staff: a rare occurrence in an environment with shift working. It can be very useful for the facilitator to be the same person as the staff group conductor in facilitating the 'normalisation' of information among all the staff. This will help a consensus in both the diagnostic process and the establishment of a strategy for change. It is important that the facilitator use the TBDs to facilitate the transfer of the overview and in-depth knowledge of the organisation that he, as the only person always present in the group meetings, inevitably acquires. This 'omniscience' can easily became persecutory to the staff and threatening to authority and power structures in the organisation if not shared more widely. Exactly how this is done without compromising confidentiality is open to debate.

The advantages of the same facilitation for both PDGs and TBDs are clear. However, there is no reason why occasionally an outside facilitator could not be used; indeed, this would become essential if difficulties emerged between the facilitator and the groups themselves.

The role of the facilitator

I work in an integrative way drawing upon psychoanalytic, sociological and systems theoretical perspectives. From psychoanalysis I take the setting and the boundaries, the Freudian unconscious, transference and counter-transference, notions of internal object relations, unconscious fantasy, psychic defences, all of which manifest in current relationships. From the sociological perspective comes the view that the Self and the Mind are pre-eminently social constructs which only come into being and develop in a social context.

Self-knowledge comes from reflective intersubjectivity. Systems theory, applied to the social level, predicts that any group of people will tend to assign roles to one another and to fit in with one another's expectations so as to minimise conflict and dissonance, that is by accepting and projecting transferences within the group. The analytic work involves recognising the patterns, as they are repeated over time, and inquiring into the unconscious assumptions and prejudices that sustain them. Many of these will become apparent through the parallel process operating in both the group and the organisational context in which it operates, which we would acknowledge and explore as appropriate.

Effective facilitation of PDGs requires that the facilitator receives good supervision him- or herself. The most important part of supervision lies within the relationship itself. I see it as a restorative space, a play space where curiosity can allow us to explore alternative perspectives. The cost of ensuring good group practice will be repaid by better staff morale and improved patient care. I insisted on having my supervision outside of the Trust itself and paid for through the mental health budget. I believe that this is essential, as an important part of the role is to interpret organisational culture; this is very difficult to achieve if the facilitator becomes too bound up within the culture.

A basic tenet of this work is that a PDG can encourage staff to explore and modify the anxieties experienced in the work setting by allowing them to be felt and expressed in a safe contained environment. The role of the facilitator is to maintain a boundary between inside and outside, in oneself and in others. This is made more difficult if the facilitator is part of the organisational culture himself or herself. However, there are also advantages to belonging to the organisation in terms of understanding the culture, but it requires discipline and frequent reflection through the supervisory process to maintain effective boundaries. The art is to belong but at the same time to keep a separateness and autonomy. Belonging allows for greater understanding of organisational processes and the opportunity to demystify the facilitator's role whilst a degree of separateness and autonomy contributes to maintaining confidential credibility. This model of 'inside/outside' is one which all members of an organisation, especially leaders and managers, struggle with. The facilitator can aim to be a role model for a role which many find very difficult to maintain.

Setting up the groups

The groups grew out of my work with the community mental health teams (CMHTs) where I had been working for the previous three years. These had proved a great success and in May 1997 there was a suggestion that facilitated staff groups be introduced to the Acute Admissions Unit. This consisted of a twelve-bed intensive care ward and two acute admissions wards.

It was not clear that a model successfully used with a CMHT would easily transfer to an in-patient setting with severe staff shortages and high turnover (Milton and Davison 1997). Staff groups on acute wards have always been seriously handicapped by these factors and particularly by shift systems that can ensure that the actual membership of a group session is rarely if ever duplicated.

In view of the evident problems on the In-patient Unit, where communication between disciplines was poor and multidisciplinary working was an aspiration rather than a reality, it was clear that my input would need to be more intensive and the structure of my interventions more robust. I started by meeting the senior staff on the unit to ensure their wholehearted support for the project. Without that the staff groups, which were named professional development groups as another way of validating the intervention, would never be sanctioned for use by the staff in general.

The team leaders were keen on the idea of a staff group but also asked for supervision for themselves on an individual basis. I was able to offer them 30 minutes a week each. They were free to use the time in whatever way they found most useful and each brought a variety of clinical and team-related issues.

Next I met the ward staff. Some people had had unfortunate experiences in a previous staff group that had been used in a punitive way by previous members of the team and they were reluctant to risk exposing themselves again. Others were concerned about confidentiality and how information from the group might leak into their personal files and affect future job references. None the less, there was a general agreement to give the group a chance. An obvious difficulty which emerged was that all the teams wanted their group to meet at staff handover – a practical impossibility for a facilitator incapable of being in two places at once. The team leaders resolved this by extending the handover period for 30 minutes once a week and crediting the staff with the time, which they could 'take back' during the week. I found myself running two groups of an hour each back to back, which was not ideal.

Both ward groups consisted only of nursing staff when they began. Innocently I enquired about other members of the multidisciplinary team. Oh yes. They had been informed about the group. Later the consultant psychiatrists let it be known, through managerial channels, that they felt excluded and were angry that they had not been asked to join. They had learned of the groups' existence because, when they contacted the ward during the group time, they had been informed that no permanent member of staff was available! The ward at this time was 'minded' by agency staff.

With hindsight I should have met up with each of the multidisciplines, treating the leaders of each discipline with the same care as the team leaders. However one may interpret the invitation that was not heard, it was a vivid enactment of the difficulties in communication across disciplines in the unit.

The facilitator also keeps an attendance register and goes through the list at the beginning of each group. This has developed into quite an important ritual as it cements the membership of the group and allows the facilitator and also the staff members present to know whether staff absences are due to days off, illness, study leave or attending to other duties. It also enables the facilitator to establish patterns of behaviour amongst group members. If group members frequently absent themselves from the group the facilitator offers to meet them individually to discuss their lapsed membership. This has happened more often with the medical and administrative staff, who suffer less peer pressure than the nurses. The effect of these meetings has frequently been positive and they are perceived as caring rather than punitive.

After two years all three groups are fully established with nurses, doctors, managers, arts' therapists and administrators attending. Amongst the nurses, few have opted to stay out and agency nurses staff the ward during group time, which has become sacred. Sometimes the nurses have to leave the group suddenly to answer alarm calls, perhaps patients resent all the staff disappearing from the ward environment and take the opportunity to express their disapproval by 'acting out'. Confidentiality has been seen to be maintained and communication structures outside of the group are improving.

Themes and perspectives

At the first meeting of each group the facilitator re-explored the group boundaries again, especially those of confidentiality, and reminded group members of the form they had signed agreeing to the boundaries of the group.

All the groups meet on the wards as it as not felt practical to meet elsewhere in case a crisis occurs that needs more than the agency staff to cope with it. In some of the early groups time was taken up by staff reflecting on the difficulties that the ward had faced in the past. It seemed important that the facilitator had an understanding of how 'shitty' life had been. The groups initially found it difficult to form, and group members would often act surprised to see me on the wards. I sensed that they were struggling to allow themselves to engage or perceive that the group could have any sense of permanence. It somehow reflected the impermanence of the clients and their defence against engaging with them.

The early groups were more like crisis intervention groups and often reflected the denial, chaos and avoidance on the wards. In December 1997, I decided to become proactive in response to the absence of the medical staff and met with them myself. I also decided to attend two ward rounds in an attempt to break down any barriers. As the group has become established the senior staff have been both supportive and influential in the development of the group.

Military metaphors dominated the group's discourse at a time when major changes were affecting the clinical teams. Staff were frequently attacked on the wards and agency nurses were brought in to fill the gaps left by injured or traumatised nurses. The staff described the wards as a 'war zone', saying they felt themselves to be 'under siege'. Concurrently they spoke of losing their 'General' who was seconded to the Department of Health.

In this way the patients on the ward were apparently enacting a fantasy endemic in the culture of the organisation, where the staff felt embattled, attacked from within and without. This was highlighted by the behaviour of one particular patient who felt that the ward staff were responsible for her predicament and her suffering. She inflicted quite serious injuries on some staff members, especially those who got close to her. Interestingly, staff seemed reluctant to express feelings about these attacks, as they didn't want to be seen to blame the patients for their behaviour; although a debate as to whether patients were mad or bad emerged.

Managing beds became an issue that united the groups and helped cohesion, as common enemies in the form of the Health Commission and the demanding patients emerged. It appeared that a strange powerlessness emerged because they were responsible for containing all the madness in a defined number of beds but had no control over the number of presenting patients. Hence, large numbers of patients, those perceived to be less mad, were transferred to private beds. They began to see themselves as more of a multidisciplinary team and explored how they seemed to collude with the system by trying to juggle too many patients into too few beds.

The wards also had to cope with high levels of illicit drug-taking by patients. The facilitator suggested that some patients seemed to choose their own form of treatment which they may have felt had fewer side-effects. The groups struggled with this issue as it reflected some of the futility of their work: they would often see patients improve only to deteriorate again when they were allowed home with freer access to their own brand of drugs.

It emerged in one of the groups that there were defensive splits amongst the staff that seemed to be an attempt to cope with the splitting off within the patients. This was the only group that some of the nurses chose to boycott, forming instead their own sub-group. Over time this sub-group has become smaller as these staff members have left the organisation and have been replaced by new staff who have opted into the group. The groups themselves feel a safer, more contained space. Learning to work on boundary issues within the groups has enabled them to implement changes to the boundaries in the ward itself.

The staff groups have become a forum for the expression of feelings and a safe place where they can explore the possibilities of change. The groups have become an important part of the ward weekly routine and, as more permanent staff fill the vacancies, the issue of who will stay out and look after the ward has emerged. The staff have become more sophisticated in the use of the group time, which has led to the groups exploring quite complex issues. Often members will hold on to issues until the group meets. The group members come from varying cultures and this has enriched the groups. The staff have made a real commitment to attend and use the groups in a constructive way, and feedback given to the facilitator when staff moved on to other posts has mostly been very positive. When the group breaks for facilitator absences these are now acknowledged.

Being oneself in the presence of others has been a struggle for some members who have struggled to leave their position in the hierarchy outside. However, the facilitator has attempted to act as a role model. Because of the high staff turnover, the groups are constantly changing and this prevents them becoming stale as new blood brings new ideas and a lot of time is spent exploring beginnings and endings which in busy acute settings might otherwise be lost. This increases the amount of time that the facilitator needs to spend meeting and settling new members, which has resource implications.

Discussion

In the two years this model of intervention has been in place, the Mental Health Unit has seen changes for the better. Recruitment and retention of staff has improved, reducing the need for agency staff. A downward trend in absence due to sickness suggests that permanent staff have been less stressed. The wards were once again able to take nursing students on placement, five of whom returned as permanent staff after qualification. From having had a problematic reputation within the locality, the unit successfully bid for an increase of establishment.

The PDGs have flourished, becoming truly multidisciplinary. The reduction in agency staff now presents a practical problem: no one wants to be left out to mind the ward during their 'sacred time'. Communication within the nursing teams, between wards and among disciplines has greatly improved. As therapists, doctors, managers and administrators began to attend regularly, members of the different professional groupings were in a position to understand better each others roles within the organisation and to hear the different perspectives they brought to the primary task and the wider institution (Rance 1998b). The culture changed from one of blame and helplessness to one of problem-solving and respect for what each profession can contribute.

In my view this positive outcome can be attributed to three inter-related aspects of my role, for which I have not yet devised a satisfactory term. First, I took active steps to direct the culture of the PDGs, the most significant of which was the practice of meeting each prospective member to explain the purpose of the group and the basic rules, to which they had to subscribe. These were simple:

- Members are expected to be respectful towards other members at all times.
- Group members were required to 'own' their statements, for example: 'you make me feel' must be rephrased 'I feel'. I did not hesitate to interrupt people in mid-sentence to reinforce this.
- If group members broke confidentiality of the group I would withdraw facilitation. If any apparent breaches of confidentiality came to light I would take them very seriously to see if they could be repaired. This might require discussion with the culprit outside the group meeting itself.

With regard to confidentiality, a central feature of my role was the maintenance of boundaries of both self and the group – 'dynamic administration'. I believe it was important that I belonged to the Trust, in the sense that I had a contract of employment with it specifying my work with groups, counselling supervision and team-building. I shared an office with the team leaders and claimed the freedom to have an individual relationship with all members of the group, especially if they dropped out without discussion. This placed quite a burden of confidential boundaries on me, as it was sometimes difficult to remember the source of all the information I acquired in each aspect of my role. Therefore I had to adopt very clear rules for myself in role at all times. This generally meant avoiding mentioning anything that had not been raised by others in the current individual or group conversation.

My role did indeed give me a bird's eye view of the unit and inevitably I was perceived as occupying a powerful position, which might have been a threat to the various leaders and professional groupings. This was mitigated to some extent by my position being outside any of the existing disciplines and therefore having no place in the hierarchies of management or leadership. Providing that I refused to participate in management structures or take on a leadership role, but instead recognised the special responsibilities of the team leaders through counselling supervision, this appeared to be enough to hold the tension. There were however other tensions caused by my resistance to intermittent attempts at management leverage over my day-to-day functioning, prompted, I suspect, by my perceived and envied independence.

Staff groups run along more traditional lines (Moylan in Obholzer and Roberts 1994; and Milton and Davison 1997) often run into difficulties in distressed teams precisely because the staff are anxious and demoralised. Unreasonable expectations that the group facilitator will magically make things better are quickly dispelled as the staff inevitably re-enact the problems they cannot solve. This can be helpful in diagnosing the malaise, but there is a danger that the patient may die before a cure can be found. There is always the temptation that, when faced with the frustration and anxiety of having to look at the problems, a group will locate them all in the facilitator in the hope that in attacking him they will rid themselves of the problems. Facilitators can find that scapegoating directed at themselves is difficult to process in the group. The identification and resolution of maladaptive projections onto various organisational figures both in the group and in the wider organisation is an important task for the group members.

By emphasising the function of the group as a place where every member of the team has a responsibility to use it as a learning experience (the management of oneself in the presence of others and the fostering of the art of conversation in the context of collaborative problem-solving) and where mutual support arises as a byproduct of working together effectively rather than being the primary aim of the group, expectations can be brought to a more realistic level.

Context within an organisation plays an important role in the success of such groups because it would be quite easy for seniors to sabotage the groups if they were to feel threatened by their existence. For this reason managers need to participate within the groups themselves, as they often feel unsupported within the culture of the NHS. Those who are attracted to caring for others often find it difficult to allow others to care for them. The present NHS culture is often one of quantity rather than quality and this does not encourage reflection and personal growth. However, with Trusts directly competing for fewer skilled staff, those that offer PDGs, counselling supervision and team-building days may find recruitment and retention easier.

Appendix 6.1

Professional development group boundaries

1   Members elect to join the group and are expected to attend every meeting unless they are on holiday, sick leave or study leave.
2   Members unable to attend are responsible for notifying the facilitator prior to the group meeting.
3   The group is open to all staff members providing they agree to maintain the group boundaries.
4   If members wish to leave the group they need to give notice and are encouraged to attend four groups following this announcement.
5   The group meetings will be open-ended and no prior agenda will be set.
6   Members are expected to be respectful towards other members at all times and to own their feelings.
7   Members are expected to treat all matters within the group as confidential.

Role of the facilitator

1   To meet with all prospective group members and explore the group boundaries with them prior to their joining the group.
2   To keep a membership and attendance list.
3   To assist the group in maintaining and encouraging adherence to the agreed boundaries.

I would like to be a member of the Professional Development Group and agree to maintain the above boundaries.

Name (print) . . . .   Job . . . .

Title . . . .

Signature . . . .   Date . . . .

References

Borrill, C.S., Wall, T.D., West, M.A., Hardy, G.E., Shapiro, D.A., Carter, A., Golya, D.A. and Haynes, C.E. (1996) *Mental Health of the Workforce in NHS Trusts: Phase 1. Final Report*, Sheffield: University of Sheffield Institute of Work Psychology.

Hirschhorn, L. (1988) *The Workplace Within*, London: MIT Press.

Johns, C.C. (1993) 'Professional Supervision', *Journal of Clinical Management* **1**: 18–19.

Martin, P.A. (1994) *The Effects of Counselling Training on the Public Sector Managers*, MSc dissertation, University of Surrey.

Milton, J. and Davison, S. (1997) 'Observations of Staff Support Groups with Time-limited External Facilitation in a Psychiatric Institution', *Psychoanalytic Psychotherapy* **11**: 135–45.

Obholzer, A. and Roberts, V.Z. (eds) (1994) *The Unconscious at Work: Individual and Organisational Stress in the Human Service*, London: Routledge.

Parry, G. (1996) *NHS Psychotherapy Services in England: A Review of Strategic Policy*, London: NHS Executive.

Rance, C.K. (1998a) 'Organizations in the Mind: the Interaction of Organisational and Intrapsychic Perspectives', in Sally Hardy *et al.* (eds), *Occupational Stress: Personal and Professional Approaches*, Cheltenham, UK: Stanley Thorne.

Rance, C.K. (1998b) 'The Art of Conversation: the Group Analytic Paradigm and Organisational Consultancy', *Group Analysis* **31** (4): 519–31.

Robertson, S. and Davison, S. (1997) 'A Survey of Groups within a Psychiatric Hospital', *Psychoanalytic Psychotherapy* **11**: 95–121.

Thomas, P. (1995) 'Staff Support Groups: a Luxury or Necessity? A Study of the Effectiveness of Staff Support Groups', *Nursing Times* **91**: 36–9.

Chapter 7

Staff counselling in a hospital setting

Alison Jesson

Introduction

In this chapter I cite some of the arguments in favour of staff counselling as a necessity in hospital settings and explore how the psychodynamics of the organisation affects the physical and mental well-being of the employees. I then explore how the organisational culture influences the counselling process and how this may be acted out within the therapeutic relationship. I describe the steps taken in the formation of a staff counselling service within a large hospital trust, and finally the pros and cons of in-house counselling services as opposed to an external employee assistance programme (EAP).

Current research has shown that staff working in the NHS have significantly higher stress levels than similar occupational groups (Moore 1996). A study of the mental health of the workforce in the NHS (Firth-Cozens 1996) showed that 27 per cent of staff reported significant psychological distress, compared to 18 per cent in other occupations, as measured by the British Household Panel Survey. Staff with the highest stress levels were nurses, doctors and managers. A large postal survey of nurses (Hingley and Harris 1986) showed that the stressors could be divided into five main categories:

- factors intrinsic to the job: for example, coping with death, work overload, rapid and unplanned changes, unsocial hours, and so on;
- relationships at work: for example, lack of support from peers, sexism, racism, delegation;
- role within the organisation: for example, lack of job clarity, conflicting demands, being promoted from a caring role to a managerial role without sufficient training;
- career development: for example, limited career prospects, fears of redundancy;

- home/work interface: for example, taking work problems home, working hours, managing childcare within shift systems.

In addition to these main stressors, the rapid changes and reorganisations that have been a feature of the health service for the last 20 years have exacerbated the situation. Unfortunately, due to the culture of the NHS, staff are expected to cope regardless of the pressure. Those who are perceived by their colleagues as not coping may be labelled 'unprofessional'. Doctors, by virtue of their highly esteemed role and professional qualifications, are especially fearful that any admission of vulnerability or illness will affect their reputation amongst their colleagues and influence their future employment prospects (Brandon and Oxley 1997). The work ethic in medicine demands long hours, hard work and unflagging dedication.

The costs of a stressed workforce have been well documented, both in terms of the individual staff, the effects on patient care and the costs to the organisation as a whole (Cooper 1989; NASS 1992; Owen 1993). Many Trusts within the health service have now acknowledged that stress is a significant problem for all staff. However, in a recent survey (Katz 1998), of the 115 Trusts (acute, community and mental health) which responded, only one in five had a stress management strategy. The main obstacles appeared to be lack of commitment at the top levels and lack of money.

In the late 1980s the National Association for Staff Support within Health Care Services (NASS) was formed. Its aim was to provide healthcare personnel with the necessary tools with which to improve staff support in their places of work, and in the longer term to influence the NHS culture as a whole:

> Staff support, in its broadest sense, comprises the full range of employment policies, procedures, strategies and values that, effectively operated, will combine to make every member of staff perform efficiently, remain highly motivated and achieve a sense of being valued as an individual.
>
> (NASS 1990: 4)

Staff support is seen to encompass a wide range of activities including:

- personal emotional support for individuals in any kind of stressful situation;
- creating and maintaining satisfactory working environments within a good management structure;

- helping individuals to achieve a sense of well-being and value;
- assisting staff to recognise stressful situations and be aware of their responses;
- providing an organised system of staff support and creating a caring culture that acknowledges the need for support as a positive coping strategy.

(NASS 1990)

Staff counselling is only one of a range of interventions for supporting staff. In the survey by Katz (1998) 76 per cent of the Trusts that responded had some form of staff counselling. This ranged from staff within the human resources department being available to discuss work problems, a hospital chaplaincy service, and occupational health doctors or nurses to qualified counsellors and psychologists specifically employed to see staff.

The latest NHS White Paper (Secretary of State for Health 1997) has emphasised the need for a healthy workforce in order to achieve high-quality patient care. A ten-point plan for improving staff health has been produced by the Nuffield Report (1998), which recommends that confidential counselling services and stress management should be available to all staff. The NHS executive has decided that staff counselling is a necessity, not a luxury.

The benefits of any staff counselling service will be determined by the philosophy behind it and the process by which it is introduced and subsequently accepted by the organisation and the culture. Any organisation consists of individuals working within a system. The NHS is a particularly complicated system due to many factors, but especially due to the nature of the work, the types of individuals doing the work, the historical background of its creation, and the more recent organisational changes which have occurred as a reflection of the world-wide culture; for example, the change into operating a market economy, involving competition in order to provide cost effective healthcare.

As a living and changing system, all these factors need to be taken into account when assessing the physical and mental health of the employees and consequently the effect on a staff counselling service. Before discussing how a staff counselling service in the NHS works, it is useful to examine how some of these organisational factors have a direct effect on those staff who may request counselling, and the attitudes of staff towards each other.

The nature of the work

Looking after sick and dying people is inherently stressful and often staff are quite unprepared for the impact that this has on them. With the enormous progress made in medicine, a greater variety of treatments are now available and this has resulted in more technology, more machinery and more complicated procedures, though not always with a corresponding increase in resources. The changes in technology have also meant more efficient and effective treatments requiring much shorter stays in hospital. Patient turnover has therefore significantly increased. It is not uncommon for a nurse to discharge a patient from a bed in the morning, admit a new patient into it for day surgery, and then a third patient in the evening into the same bed. Since patients who are discharged often still need medical and nursing care, the community staff have a larger case load of more dependent patients.

Patients themselves have also changed. With the advent of the Patient's Charter, patients now tend to be more vociferous in demanding their rights, object to long waiting times, and write more letters of complaint. Consequently staff are continually expected to update their skills and work faster, which leads some to feel that they are failing or inadequate, and others to become less and less satisfied with the quality of care they are able to give. Some of the staff who request counselling believe they are failing the system, whereas others believe that the system is failing them.

The type of individuals doing the work

The health service has traditionally attracted people of great sensitivity who want to be involved with caring for others. Their ability to receive care themselves is frequently lacking. Many nurses operate from what is described by Steiner (1974) as the 'Nurses' Script'. They try not to show others what they are feeling or to ask for their own needs to be met, but are willing to take care of the needs of others. Steiner describes the nurse as:

> a professional Rescuer, who works in an institution that exploits her and pushes her to her physical limits. Initially her motivation to help others comes from caring, but caring soon becomes oppressive to her. She is taught skilfully to intuit other people's needs and take care of them. But then she wants her needs to be filled in a like manner ... but it doesn't happen; she doesn't ask for what she wants so she doesn't get it. ... After too much Rescuing she becomes hurt and angry.

Freudenberger (1975), who first coined the term 'burnout', identifies three personality types found amongst healthcare employees which predispose to burnout. These are the 'dedicated and committed personality' who seeks to earn 'OK'-ness by her service to others; the 'over committed and work-enmeshed personality' – whose only source of strokes is from work; and the 'authoritarian and/or patronising personality' – who can only feel OK by controlling and dominating others.

This combination of the stressful nature of the work and the individual personality types results in a variety of defence mechanisms which are supported by the organisational culture. Menzies-Lyth (1959) in her now classic study of the social defence mechanisms in nursing, identified some of the processes which operate at an unconscious level as a result of the interplay between individual and organisational anxiety. The most common include: projection or blaming by making others responsible for one's feelings; splitting by dividing colleagues and patients into the 'good guys and the bad guys'; idealisation by overvaluing the old ways of working in order not to have to experience feelings of loss; using cynicism as a way of avoiding shame and guilt; and finally, immobilisation by resisting change and blocking any attempts at creative problem-solving. These defences evolve over time and become part of the culture into which newcomers are expected to fit. This has been described by Smythe (1984) as the 'Stagnant Quo' where any change is perceived as threatening and is resisted because the staff don't feel they have enough energy to adapt to the change. Staff who recognise their own need for support or counselling often feel very ashamed that they are not coping as well as they perceive their colleagues to be.

The changing face of the health service: 50 years of change

The health service has always been hierarchical by nature, with clear lines of authority which traditionally were not challenged. In the earlier days of the NHS, staff roles and responsibilities were clear and discipline was strong. Staff were expected to have great loyalty to the organisation and not to question those in power. In the medical profession, promotion depended on who you knew and what sort of an impression you had made in your previous post. Bullying was a fact of life and if staff couldn't cope then they were clearly in the wrong job. This tradition of subservience, and consequently passivity, has underpinned the evolving culture. The need to appear to be coping regardless of the pressure has resulted in counselling services being seen as being provided only for 'the weak' or for those who don't fit in.

More recently the very rapid changes in the management of the health service in order to compete within the market economy has resulted in massive changes in every aspect of its operation. Now Trusts compete with each other for contracts, departments compete with each other for funds, wards compete with each other for equipment, and members of staff perceived to be working below maximum efficiency are subject to extra-close scrutiny to discover the reasons. As Trusts merge with each other to become more efficient and save money, increasing numbers of very well qualified staff, who had once imagined they had a job for life, find themselves applying for their own jobs and working within short-term contracts. Consequently there are high levels of insecurity and a loss of identity.

With the requirement for an increase in efficiency with little increase in resources, a 'busy' culture has evolved. This is described by Bond (1986) as a vicious circle of frantic activity or busyness which is maintained even when there are natural lulls. The frantic activity creates tiredness and a loss of effectiveness. Mistakes are made which create more work and consequently staff become busier in an everlasting attempt to catch up; hence breakfast meetings, staying late on duty, coming to work on days off in order to help out when there are insufficient staff, or taking work home. The busy syndrome is subtly transmitted to all staff as the norm and what is expected of them. There is often a sense of 'one-upmanship' as to who stayed latest in the office or came in at the weekend, as if it were something to be envied.

The staff counselling service in an NHS setting will be therefore influenced by the interplay between the organisational culture and the individuals who create and maintain the culture. In contrast to counselling in private practice, where the dynamic is solely between the client and the counsellor, in an organisational setting there is the additional component of the organisation itself. When the client (that is, the staff member) comes to see the counsellor (who is also likely to be a staff member in that he or she is employed by the organisation to provide the counselling service), they will be reflecting in some way their own perception of their experience of working in this organisation. The counsellor will also have his/her own perceptions of working in the organisation.

In addition the organisation may single out individuals who become the 'containers' for larger unacknowledged problems within the organisation itself: 'Within organisations it is often easier to ascribe a staff member's behaviour to personal problems rather than to discover its link to the institutional dynamics' (Halton 1994).

Consequently, the staff counsellor needs to be aware that what the client may be telling him/her is in fact a reflection of wider organisational issues. For example, Mary, a ward sister, talked about feeling undermined and unsupported by her junior staff. As she talked about her feelings of helplessness and depression, it became clear that she in turn gave no support to her senior nurse, and knew that her senior felt unsupported by the manager above. Thus throughout this chain of command there was little respect or support either up or down the hierarchy. She was in fact voicing the feelings of her entire department. Similarly, Jane, a junior nurse, was 'sent' for counselling by her manager after she had been disciplined for making a drug error. She felt that the error was due to her feeling overstretched as a result of severe staff shortages on her ward.

The 'three cornered contract' (English 1975; Hay 1992; Micholt 1992) provides a useful model for understanding the relationships and contracts that exist between each of the three parties and the overt and covert agendas which will operate between them (Figure 7.1). Three types of contract exist between each of the three parties:

- an administrative contract;
- a professional contract;
- a psychological contract.

Figure 7.1 The three cornered contract

Contracts between the organisation and the clients (members of staff)

Administrative

The staff are employed by the organisation to provide, or contribute towards, patient care. They are paid a salary, have a contract of employment, the right to work in a healthy and safe environment and to belong to a trade union.

Professional

The professional contract relates to the aim of the work to be done. The organisation expects its staff to conduct themselves professionally at all times, to adhere to established codes of ethics and conduct, and to keep themselves updated. In terms of a staff counselling service, the organisation provides this service for the staff, often as part of a package of health and welfare, on the understanding that the staff will use it in order to resolve any difficulties they may be experiencing and thus continue to perform effectively and efficiently.

Psychological

This is the unconscious contract which will always influence the other two. This is where any psychological games and transference will be acted out. For example, the unconscious messages between the organisation and the staff may include:

'These new changes are designed to help you, it's all for your own good.'

'But you managers should see how hard you are making us work.'

Ideally, in a healthy system, the three cornered contract shown in Figure 7.1 is an equilateral triangle in which the distance between the three parties is perceived by each as equal. The contracts, expectations and role definitions are clear, and there is openness and co-operation.

Contracts between the organisation and the staff counsellor

Administrative

Currently in the NHS, some counsellors are bought in on a sessional basis, some are employed as part of an EAP (employee assistance programme) and some are directly employed by the organisation, as part of occupational health. In each case there will be a contract of employment and a negotiated fee. Accommodation varies from a designated room in the occupational health department to a small room tucked away in a building in a corner of the grounds. Where the staff counsellor is located is often a clear message about the perceived value of and necessity for the service.

Professional

This will include all the negotiated details of how the counselling will be done, including how many sessions clients may receive; what sorts of issues can be dealt with; what the limits to confidentiality might be; required feedback about organisational issues in order to help the organisation change; required statistical information; methods of referral; publicity and so on. It will also include the multiple roles that the counsellor is expected to take on, including counselling, training, supervising, debriefing, researching, and income generating.

Psychological

The underlying feelings about having a staff counselling service may be *overtly* expressed to the counsellor by some managers or occupational health doctors in a variety of ways:

'I hope my staff won't tell you dreadful things about me.'

'Thank goodness we can refer the most stressed staff to you.'

'As manager I have a right to know which of my staff are on antidepressants.'

'We expect the counselling service to deal with the causes of stress, not just to mop up.'

The *covert* messages may include:

'Make sure we don't have any really "crazy" staff working here.'

'You must make a success of this service or we will close it/you down.'

'It's the staff who need counselling who have the problem, not the organisation.'

Contracts between the staff counsellor and the clients

Administrative

This will include how the service is run generally, including publicity, methods for making appointments, privacy, confidentiality and its limits, which issues can be brought for counselling, for example, work-based or personal.

Professional

The staff counsellor is likely to be a professionally trained person who understands the psychodynamics of helping organisations such as the NHS. They may provide the client with a philosophy of their practice, and the professional contract between them and the client will include sharing goals and expectations; discussing what counselling is and is not; the limits of confidentiality; and the extent of any feedback (if the client was referred by a manager or the occupational health department).

Psychological

As soon as the client makes contact with the counsellor, the unconscious processes begin to operate in the counselling relationship. The client may have been referred as part of a disciplinary procedure and the counsellor may be seen as a friend, an ally against the organisation, or as yet another person who is going to misunderstand and blame them. There is often serious mistrust of the confidentiality of the counselling process. Health professionals are used to discussing very personal details about patients within the multidisciplinary team and may assume that when they become patients, that is clients, they will be discussed in a similar fashion. Many fear that information will be passed on to the occupational health department and kept on their files. Although some staff see the counsellor as positive and to some degree as a neutral person who is 'outside' the organisation, others are mistrustful as a result of the 'bitching and splitting' defence which is an integral part of the culture. In addition, the client may unconsciously attempt to use the counsellor to influence the management on his/her behalf, using the counselling sessions as an opportunity to complain, while remaining passive and thus reinforcing feelings of helplessness.

Psychological distance

Ideally the psychological distance (the perceived closeness or distance) between each of the relationships in the three cornered contract should be equal. However, as Micholt (1992) has pointed out, this is frequently not the case. When distortions occur, the unconscious processes of the psychological contract will undermine both the professional and administrative contracts.

If, for example, the psychological distance between the organisation and the staff counsellor is perceived as being too close by the clients, there may well be serious mistrust of the counselling service, which will be seen as being too closely aligned to the management (see Figure 7.2). There may be fears about confidentiality, especially if the client was referred for counselling by their manager. Negative feelings towards the management will be enacted in the counselling room as negative transference towards to counsellor. Alternatively, during a session, the counsellor may attempt to defend the organisation from the client's negative projections and in so doing will reduce the level of trust the client may have put in the counsellor thus damaging the therapeutic alliance.

On the other hand, if the organisation perceives too close an alignment between the clients and the staff counsellor (see Figure 7.3), it may feel undermined or threatened by the counsellor and want to exert more control over the counselling service in attempt to avoid being scapegoated or blamed. Alternatively there may be some unconscious envy that the clients have someone who is willing to listen and understand them, whereas the managers feel alienated and unappreciated.

A third possible distortion may occur if the organisation and the client seem too closely aligned and the counsellor feels out on a limb. This could occur if the staff counselling service is not provided by in-house counsellors, but by an external employee assistance programme

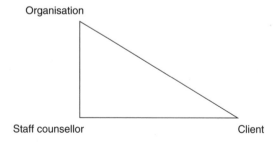

Figure 7.2 Counsellor perceived as being too closely allied to the organisation

Figure 7.3 Client and counsellor perceived as being too closely aligned

(EAP) where it is felt by both the organisation and the clients that the specific problems of working within the NHS are not really understood.

It is thus essential that staff counsellors in a hospital settings take all the dynamics of the three cornered contract into account both before and after establishing staff counselling services. There is great satisfaction to be had for the counsellor who is able to manage the three cornered contract well, by confronting and working with the distortions within the relationship and thus achieving a win–win situation between all three parties.

As Fisher (1997) quotes from a participant (a staff counsellor), in her study of employee counselling in the NHS:

> it's all about boundaries and containment, I use these words time and time again. Containing the clients' and the counsellor's issues within this department . . . and having clearly defined contracts and bound-aries with the organisation and the clients is absolutely essential.

The creation of a staff counselling service

I shall now briefly describe the creation and operation of a staff coun-selling service in a large teaching hospital Trust.

In 1991 a group of staff, who were already engaged in counselling staff on an *ad hoc* basis as part of their existing roles, formed a steering group and developed the following objectives:

- to establish a culture in which the appropriateness and value of staff support is recognised;
- to identify the means of support which will enable healthcare personnel to carry out their work efficiently and effectively, and with satisfaction;

- to co-ordinate the organised delivery of staff support services;
- to ensure that the availability and confidentiality of staff support services is made known to all healthcare personnel;
- to monitor the provision of staff support for standards of good practice;
- to promote research and evaluation of staff support.

Membership of the steering group consisted of chaplains, staff from the human resources (personnel) department, the occupational health consultant, psychotherapists in mental health, and some counsellors who had been employed to see specific groups of patients and who also saw staff informally. In order to appraise the need for staff counselling, an application was made to the Special Trustees to fund a part-time 'co-ordinator/counsellor' whose job would be to assess staff who requested counselling and then refer them to a team of in-house counsellors, who would set aside time from their current jobs to offer short-term counselling. After the first year of this arrangement, although the percentage of staff who actually contacted the service was low, it became clear that there were more clients requesting counselling than there were staff available to offer counselling. In addition it was evident that only one aspect of staff support, namely counselling, was being addressed. In spite of this being a time of severe financial cutbacks, the Hospital Trust agreed to fund two part-time counsellors who would not only provide individual counselling, but also work with the organisation to develop the wider issues of staff support.

Although the service is currently funded by the occupational health department, and in fact receives many of its referrals from this department, clear boundaries concerning confidentiality are maintained. Over the last few years that the service has been operating, the staff counsellors have had to work hard to create good lines of communication with managers and provide them with feedback concerning the themes and issues that arise in counselling sessions without identifying individuals unless permission has been given. Efforts are continuously made to keep the perceived psychological distances in the three cornered contract as equal as possible. In order to demystify the process of counselling and attempt to influence the 'Don't admit you can't cope' culture, the counselling service is promoted as one of a range of supportive interventions offered for staff by the Trust, along with back care, health and safety at work, and ongoing education and training. There has been a slow, steady increase in the numbers of clients accessing the service, presenting with a mixture of both personal and work-related problems. Staff are seen for short-term counselling on the whole, though each client's needs are assessed individually. Those who require on-going counselling are referred to a network of local counsellors who can offer both private and low-cost arrangements. The staff support service is working well, although with a constantly changing staff population it has to be constantly advertised and promoted.

The advantages and disadvantages of in-house counselling versus an external employee assistance programme (EAP)

Since the Nuffield Report (1998) has recommended that counselling and stress management should be available to all staff, it is likely that in the future more hospital and community Trusts will follow the example set by others. Which type of service should they provide ? There are both advantages and disadvantages to choosing an in-house counselling service or an externally based EAP. These are summarised below.

Advantages of an in-house counselling service

• Easy access on site for staff before, during or after work.
• Can offer a drop-in service and more accessible follow-up support on an informal basis.
• Counsellors are perceived as being part of the staff, and therefore understand the organisation/ Hospital Trust, as well as knowing individuals.
• Counsellors can offer an entire package of staff support services including counselling, training, supervision, workshops, directly tailored to the needs of individual departments.
• Counsellors are likely to have an NHS background and therefore a good understanding of how organisational issues will effect the psychodynamics of the counselling process.
• Being in-house helps to maintain equal distances and improved communication in the three cornered contract.
• Management can more easily be provided with overall feedback about staff issues and common themes.

Disadvantages of in-house counselling service

• Counsellors maybe invited to collude, either with the clients or with the management, and will have to work hard to maintain an equal three cornered contract.

- Clients may not trust confidentiality and fear that information about them will be passed to management or occupational health.
- Clients may be anxious that they will be seen attending the staff counselling office by their colleagues.
- It is harder to evaluate the effectiveness of the counselling service without bias.

Advantages of an external EAP

- Perceived by clients as totally separate; therefore confidentiality is ensured and collusion avoided.
- A well-run EAP will have networks and contacts throughout the organisation and thus be aware of all the organisational dynamics which may affect the counselling process.
- It will probably be able to provide the hospital/community Trust with effective evaluation of the benefits of staff counselling.
- It is able to provide a complete package of support including counselling, consultancy, research, career counselling and performance management.

Disadvantages of an external EAP

- The number of sessions that clients are allowed is likely to be limited to five or six.
- The hospital/community Trust may be less likely to take responsibility or ownership of organisational issues and problems: victim blaming rather than system blaming.
- EAP counsellors are less likely to understand all the factors involved specifically within the NHS as an organisation, as mentioned earlier in the chapter.

The pros and cons of each approach to staff counselling can be argued either way, but to do so may detract from the overall goal of workplace counselling. As Orme (1997) has highlighted:

> In workplace counselling, win/win is not sufficient. The real goal of workplace counselling is in fact win/win/win – win for the individual client, win for the workplace counsellor and win for the client organisation. This third aspect adds important dimensions that the counsellor cannot ignore – the counsellor has not one but two clients (at least), and each of them has different expectations, measures,

goals, and success criteria; each has different needs for information, confidentiality and results. In turn the counsellor's needs for information, confidentiality and results will be different.

From my own experience I prefer an in-house counselling service, but in the long run what will determine the success or failure of introducing a staff counselling service in a medical setting will be the way that it is introduced, the philosophy behind it and the ongoing commitment to the growth and development of both individual staff members and the organisation as a whole.

In conclusion, support and counselling for NHS staff is still a relatively new concept. It is clear that the job of providing care for sick people is inherently stressful and that when staff feel stressed patient care is inevitably affected. In addition, the historical background, the types of individuals who are drawn to the caring professions and the rapid changes in the NHS structure have resulted in a workforce who find it hard to care for themselves. Any system of staff support which is introduced into this environment needs to take all these factors into account.

References

Bond, M. (1986) *Stress and Self Awareness: A Guide For Nurses*, London: Heinemann.

Brandon, S. and Oxley, J. (1997) 'Getting Help for Sick Doctors', *British Medical Journal* **314** (2): 2–3.

Cooper, C. (1989) *Stress, Mental Health and Job Satisfaction*, and job stress among GPs. *British Medical Journal* **298** (6670): 336–70.

English, F. (1975) 'The Three Cornered Contract', *Transactional Analysis Journal* **5**: 383–4.

Firth-Cozens, J. (1996) *The Mental Health of the NHS Workforce in NHS Trusts: Report on Current Research*, Sheffield University Institute of Work Psychology and Leeds University Psychology Department.

Fisher, H. (1997) 'A Study of Employee Counselling in the NHS', in M. Carroll and M. Walton (eds), *Handbook of Counselling in Organisations*, London: Sage.

Freudenberger, H. (1975) 'The Staff Burn-out Syndrome in Alternative Institutions', *Psychotherapy: Theory, Research and Practice* **12** (1): 35–45.

Halton, W. (1994) 'Unconscious Aspects of Organisational Life', in A. Obholzer and V.Z. Roberts (eds), *The Unconscious at Work*, London: Routledge.

Hay, J. (1992) *Transactional Analysis for Trainers*, London: McGraw-Hill.

Hingley, P. and Harris, P. (1986) 'Burn-out at Senior Level', *Nursing Times* **82**: 28–9.

Katz, S. (1998) Lack of commitment and cash are main barriers to tackling stress reveals survey. *Working Well* **8**: 16.

Menzies-Lyth, I. (1959) 'A Case Study in the Functioning of Social Systems as a Defence Against Anxiety: a Report on a Study of the Nursing Service of a General Hospital', *Human Relations* **13**: 95–121.

Micholt, N. (1992) 'Psychological Distance and Group Interventions', *Transactional Analysis Journal* **22**: 228–33.

Moore, W. (1996) 'All Stressed Up and Nowhere to Go', *Health Service Journal* **5**: 22–5.

National Association for Staff Support within Health Care Services (NASS) (1990) *Support Systems in Healthcare Settings*, no. 4, London: Channon Long & Stoter.

—— (1992) *The Costs of Stress and Benefits of Stress Management*, Briefing paper.

—— and Royal College of Nursing (RCN) (1992) *Charter for Staff Support*, London: Royal College of Nursing.

Nuffield Trust (1998) *Improving the Health of the NHS Workforce*, London: Nuffield Trust.

Orme, G. (1997) 'On Being a Chameleon: a Freelance Workplace Counsellor's Perspective', in M. Carroll and M. Walton (eds), *Handbook of Counselling in Organisations*, London: Sage.

Owen, G. (1993) 'Taking the Strain: Coping Mechanisms and Support Systems', in *Literature Review*, 5th edn, NASS.

Reddy, M. (1997) 'External Counselling Provision for Organisations', in M. Carroll and M. Walton (eds), *Handbook of Counselling in Organisations*, London: Sage.

Secretary of State for Health (1997) *The New NHS*, London: Stationery Office.

Smythe, E. (1984) *Surviving Nursing*, New York: Grune & Stratton.

Steiner, C. (1974) *Scripts People Live*, New York: Bantam.

Chapter 8

Counselling in a pain relief clinic

Maureen Williams

Introduction

This chapter explores working with patients within a multidisciplinary pain relief unit and how psychological techniques can be used to advantage alongside other forms of treatment. It looks at the advantages and disadvantages of working within a hospital setting. It highlights the difficulties encountered in treating patients who are only used to the medical model and who allow no room for the existence of psychological factors in the maintenance of their pain. The use of case presentation will demonstrate the importance of accurate assessment of personality in order to maximise compliance with both physical and psychological treatments. Issues of confidentiality within the hospital and the cost implications will be discussed.

The context

Pain is a complex experience. While there has always been pain, there have not always been pain clinics. In 1968 a senior anaesthetist at King's College Hospital began to offer a service to in-patients in severe pain. By 1972 he had set up an outpatient 'pre-anaesthetic clinic' with the stated aim of preparing surgical patients who would require difficult anaesthesia. Having gained a foothold in the outpatients department, his service could develop into his vision of a pain clinic and by the late 1970s the multidisciplinary pain team had begun to take shape. In time the pain clinic changed its name to the pain relief unit. As well as developing a pain service at King's he also began to offer a consultancy service to St Christopher's Hospice in Sydenham.

Perhaps as a result of the manner in which the pain clinic developed at King's it has continued with the approach of treating patients on an individual basis by a multidisciplinary team and not offering group therapy as is done by other centres. From the early 1980s the many research projects carried out by members of the pain team have provided funding for posts which start as research posts but that have subsequently become established clinical posts.

The pain team currently is composed of three consultant anaesthetists, two specialist registrars and four specialist nurses; these form the core of the pain team. Additionally, an acupuncturist, a neurologist and a psychiatrist offer one session a week each to the pain relief unit. I have worked as psychologist for the pain team for two sessions a week for the past 17 years. There is also access to other specialities within the hospital, for example, physiotherapy, but they are not part of the pain team. A major advantage of the large number of specialist services available for the treatment of pain patients ensures that patients receive a 'treatment package' best suited to their needs.

Referrals to the pain team are accepted from physicians and surgeons within the hospital group and from GPs. Because King's is a tertiary referral centre out-of-area patients are also seen. A service is offered to both in-patients and day patients, as well as to outpatients. About half the referrals received are from GPs and the rest are from hospital consultants. Priority is given to cancer patients, who are seen as soon as possible after referral. In-patients are also seen quickly by at least one member of the pain team. There is a waiting list for outpatient appointments. The senior specialist nurse decides the degree of urgency of referrals.

Most members of the team have only a sessional commitment to the pain team, with the exception of the specialist nurses who work solely in pain relief. All the doctors work in general anaesthetics for their other clinical sessions. This has the advantage that the anaesthetists have regular contact with physicians and surgeons in the hospital. If a pain patient requires admission to hospital a bed has to be 'borrowed' from another hospital consultant. At King's there is a major commitment to research and to teaching (both at a formal and an informal level). The King's pain team also provides a consultancy service to a local hospice (St Christopher's) and runs post-qualification courses in pain management jointly with the hospice.

The hospital specialities which are the main referrers to the pain team are rheumatology, oncology, orthopaedics, renal, liver, cardiac and the neurosciences. In the past financial year 429 new outpatients were seen and assessed by the pain team and there were 1,088 follow-up outpatient appointments; 109 patients were treated in the day surgery unit (nerve blocks, epidurals and so on); 997 patients were seen for treatments such as acupuncture or transcutaneous nerve stimulation, in addition to the 1,203 occasions when in-patients were seen by the pain team.

The King's catchment area population is very varied in both socio-economic and racial terms. Race, gender, culture and class are all known to influence the patient's perception of pain. In particular the patient's cultural background has a powerful effect on the pain perception threshold and on pain tolerance levels. Difficulties can arise when the health professional and the patient do not share a common culture. These can be even greater for those engaged in a talking therapy as opposed to a physical therapy with a patient. Research carried out by Clarkson (1998) indicates that 'issues of race and culture . . . created some difficulties, errors and even failures in counselling on a number of occasions', leaving the counsellor feeling deskilled and incompetent.

Pain

Ronald Melzack and Patrick Wall (1982), who proposed the 'gate control theory' of pain, recognised that psychological factors such as distraction, attention, personality and mood can affect and alter a person's perception of pain:

> One of the major advances in the field of pain in recent years has been the recognition that chronic, persistent pain is a distinct medical entity different from acute pain in many respects. Chronic pain becomes debilitating and often produces severe depression. Patients are beset with a sense of helplessness, hopelessness and meaninglessness. Chronic, intractable pain presents a special challenge to the physician or health professional.
>
> (Ibid.)

Prior to the referral to a pain clinic a patient may have seen many specialists, had unnecessary laboratory tests, repeated hospitalisations and polysurgery, and become 'addicted' to both prescribed drugs and to the healthcare system for social support. The patient may think that the doctor expects him/her to produce physical symptoms. The patient's high level of anxiety will have made him/her hypervigilant, leading to a closer self-examination of bodily sensations.

The main psychological characteristics of patients who complain of pain and who exhibit abnormal illness behaviour are:

- a conviction of physical illness;
- a rejection of a psychological basis for symptoms;

- an inhibition of certain feelings, especially hostility and anger;
- a disturbance of mood, usually irritability, anxiety and/or depression;
- a denial of problems in everyday life.

Patients may have a need to be ill or in pain: this allows them to depend on physicians and others to take care of them. Often patients try to avoid discussion of psychosocial topics. A person in pain will take medication, avoid normal activities and seek advice from a physician. Pain is a powerful tool that can be used to elicit social support, to control key relatives and others and to avoid intimacy. It can also be used to express anger or to avoid anxiety-provoking situations.

Doctors are dedicated to helping patients by fighting organic disease and they have a strong belief in the power of biomedical technology. Like the patients, they avoid discussion of psychosocial topics and some may have fantasies of omnipotence and omniscience. The medical model, which is a hierarchical structure, has two major problems: one is that it is often looking only at the symptoms, not at the whole person and the context in which that person lives; the other problem is that with its omniscient, omnipotent doctor it encourages patients to adopt a passive role, and many patients are happy to comply with this. Defusing a poor doctor–patient relationship and encouraging a more equal partnership using a mutual co-operation model can be an important task for the counsellor.

Counselling in medical settings

Corney (in Palmer and McMahon 1997) cites Breakwell's (1987) research which found that within thirty-nine health authorities, the job responsibilities of 32 per cent of the staff in ten professional categories were considered by their managers to 'include counselling, although counselling was less likely to be included in their job descriptions. Nurses viewed counselling as primarily non-directive, whereas doctors interpreted counselling as either advice giving or problem solving.'

There can be a tendency for other members of the multidisciplinary team to hold back from discussing psychosocial issues with a patient when a counsellor or a psychologist or a psychiatrist is part of the team. This is a waste of valuable talent. Corney states: 'In medical settings, as elsewhere, there is much confusion relating to the distinction between counselling skills and counselling.' She sees the core skills of counselling to be 'listening attentively, responding appropriately, and giving feedback responsive to the individual's needs'. A specialist nurse on the pain team will have the time and the opportunity to use these core skills at the same time as carrying out a physical treatment such as transcutaneous nerve stimulation. Part of the role of the psychologist or the counsellor is to empower other staff members to use the resources that they undoubtedly possess.

Many enter the caring professions because they themselves have experienced illness in a significant adult. They see the patient as the victim and they are the rescuer. A problem can occur when a member of the team over-identifies with a patient. This has happened with a staff member (no longer on the team) who was so distressed by how closely an elderly male patient's appearance and symptoms resembled her dead father that she was unable to continue being involved in that patient's treatment.

Chronic versus acute pain

How a patient with acute pain is handled can affect whether or not the person develops a chronic pain profile. A patient with acute pain for the first couple of months realistically expects to get better and undergoes no gross psychological changes. However, as the months pass, while s/he still hopes for a full recovery, his or her level of anxiety increases, often in conjunction with an increase in somatisation. At this stage the patient is not usually depressed.

Symonds (in Pitts and Phillips 1998) makes the important point that 'increased psychological intervention at the acute stage of pain is imperative because psychological factors do not begin to operate only when the pain becomes chronic. Our reaction to acute pain may, in some cases, actually be more important in determining rate of recovery than physiological symptoms.'

Chronic pain is usually defined as pain that has lasted for more than six months. By this stage, all treatments having failed, work and leisure activities have become curtailed and the sympathy of relatives may be exhausted. Chronic pain is a burden for the patients and also for their families. Latham (1991) writes that patients with chronic pain 'should be managed as much as possible on an outpatient basis to maintain as normal a life style as possible'.

Referral to the counsellor

When a pain patient is referred for psychological assessment and/or treatment they can feel rejected by 'real' doctors and fear that their symptoms are regarded as imaginary. They may also fear that there will be a reduction or withdrawal of medicines and that medical investigations will cease. A more sinister fear they might have is that the condition is untreatable. They can see no connection between pain and emotions and therefore resent any implication of emotional disorder.

The manner in which the referral is made is very important. Many junior staff take what is for them the easy way out and say that the psychologist will teach the patient how to relax. More experienced practitioners will explain that a two-pronged approach is being taken to the patient's pain problem (that is, both physical and psychological) and will spend a little time explaining this approach to the patient.

Pearce and Mays (in Lindsay and Powell 1997) emphasise the importance of the assessment process of pain patients both initially and throughout treatment:

1   To determine the suitability of a patient for treatment.
2   To determine the individual patient's strengths and weaknesses so as to match or tailor a treatment programme effectively.
3   To evaluate change during treatment and at follow-up periods.

Allowing time at the initial assessment to assess the personality of the patient is time well spent. Not only will it give clues as to how to maximise the patient's motivation and co-operation in treatment, but it will also prove useful if a problem arises in a staff–patient relationship, for example when conflict arises between a doctor with obsessional traits and a patient with an obsessional personality. It may be possible to defuse the situation or it may be necessary to suggest that another member of the team should treat the patient.

Reasons for referral to the counsellor

Any member of the pain team can refer a patient to the psychologist either for assessment alone or for treatment. The types of referrals made to the clinical psychologist are very varied. The major reasons for referral are discussed briefly below.

Anxiety may make the patient tense and withdrawn. Avoidance behaviour begins as the patient fears that activity will exacerbate the pain and even pleasurable activities such as hobbies will be abandoned. The level of anticipatory anxiety rises in an effort to avoid anxiety-provoking situations. The patient may experience a loss of role or might fear a loss of role in the future. It is important to know what the fears are in each patient and to teach methods of anxiety management. Relaxation training is useful in both helping to reduce the basal level of anxiety and giving some degree of control over the pain by breaking into the pain–tension cycle.

With depression a patient may experience self-hate, guilt, suicidal ideation, pessimism, self-accusation, irritability, disturbed sleep, appetite loss or more frequently an increase in weight, which further distorts the body image. It is fortunate that the tricyclic antidepressants used in small doses can be very effective in the management of pain. In chronic pain patients the clinical depression that develops as a secondary disorder to the pain can be treated successfully with larger doses of these medications. Referral on to the pain team psychiatrist may be necessary if the depression is severe.

The defence mechanism of denial makes the detection of psychological distress more difficult. Often social and psychological factors have never been examined in regard to chronic pain problems. As I was the first female staff member a young female patient had seen (all the doctors she had seen were male), she told me that she had developed hirsutism following hormone treatment for infertility. She now rose at 5 a.m. to shave her face so that her husband would not discover her secret and, using pain as an excuse, she avoided an intimate relationship with him. Clearly the baby she longed for was not going to be conceived. Helping her to disclose her problem to a male doctor enabled her to progress with her treatment.

Post-traumatic stress disorder is often missed by physicians and surgeons. A female police officer was assaulted while trying to arrest one suspect at the same time as her fellow officer was being stabbed by her assailant's accomplice. Her injuries were less severe than those of her colleague, but she continued to report pain and remained on sick leave long after her colleague had returned to work. She required treatment at a clinic specialising in the treatment of post-traumatic stress disorder. Another patient who was referred to the pain relief unit by the neurosurgeons suffered from severe daily headaches. She had been unfortunate in getting in the way of a robber running from the scene of the crime. He pushed her out of the way using a knuckleduster. After having a skull X-ray she was sent home at the insistence of the casualty consultant, contrary to the opinion of the two junior casualty doctors that she should be admitted for observation. Two weeks later she was an emergency admission and had two brain operations. The neurologist and the neurosurgeon treating her were delighted with the outcome of the surgery; neither asked her about the traumatic incident and her feelings about it and its aftermath. Her recurrent nightmares since the incident involved her being struck again, not by the robber but by the accident and emergency consultant.

While expressing positive feelings is easy, expressing bad feelings is very difficult for some patients. A patient may be angry that all treatment to date has failed, but may fear that if the anger is expressed overtly the treatment may cease altogether. There may also be anger against a spouse or an employer. In the former case marital therapy may be necessary and in the latter case assertion training or vocational guidance may be needed.

Control is an important issue. The patient feels that neither s/he is in control of the pain and nor is the doctor. When one medication has failed to work, another drug is often substituted without dealing with the patient's loss of faith.

Guilt feelings can come to light through the 'confessional' aspect of counselling pain patients. A male patient terminally ill with cancer revealed that his wife of 20 years did not know of the existence of his 8-year-old illegitimate child. He knew that the child's mother would make contact with his family on his death to demand a portion of his estate. I was asked to inform his wife about the child, but not until after his death. As a result of the news she required treatment in her own right.

Regarding payment of compensation, it is always of interest to ask patients what sum they expect to receive; the tendency is for a quite unrealistically high figure. Patients are loath to report a reduction in their experience of pain as they fear this will lead to a reduction in the level of compensation they will receive. Amusingly one patient, who had been involved in a road traffic accident and who refused to take up the advice to diet and to exercise more to improve her self-image and her poor posture which was making her back pain worse, said that she would use her compensation to pay for liposuction at a private clinic.

Grief over damage to body image affects the patient's self-image and their self-esteem. A classic example of this is the post-mastectomy patient. The damage to the body does not have to be as extreme as a mastectomy for the patient's mental state to be affected. One patient, the mother of young children, following damage to her right arm could not iron her children's school uniforms to the high standard she had previously set herself. As a result she became quite severely depressed because she felt inadequate as a mother, which in turn lowered her tolerance of pain.

The existence of an unresolved grief reaction over the loss of a loved one can also be important to ascertain. The length of time that has passed between that loss and the present is immaterial: there are cases where more than 20 years have elapsed. If the grief has not been resolved I have seen cases where the pain reported by the patient mirrors the pain that had been complained of by the dead person.

A lack of compliance with treatment is often another reason for referral. It is interesting that patients will often tell a psychologist or counsellor that they have not taken the medication as prescribed, or in quite a few cases not at all. They will not have disclosed this to the prescribing doctor as they 'do not wish to hurt the doctor's feelings'. On occasions a patient will have been frightened by the warning of the side-effects of the medication prescribed, which is information that the doctor is obliged to give them. Increasingly patients now have access to the Internet and can further inform themselves about the side-effects of a particular medication. An additional problem in regard to medication is that pain patients frequently are taking a cocktail of medications, some prescribed by the GP, some by hospital doctors and some obtained over the counter at the chemists.

Alcohol abuse is another problem that can result when a patient in pain uses alcohol initially to help him/her to get to sleep. Dependence can then occur and the patient may not be taking medication prescribed as most will carry a warning that alcohol should be avoided.

In the King's catchment area, particularly among the young, there is also a problem with the use of illicit drugs, a fact not usually disclosed to the doctors treating them. I was asked to see a 30-year-old woman, terminally ill with cancer, who was gaining little relief from the opiates she had been prescribed for her pain. In her teens she had been a heroin addict but had managed to overcome the addiction. She was the single parent of a 5-year-old daughter and she was distressed because she would not be alive when her daughter reached her teens in order to give her the guidance necessary to prevent her daughter making the mistakes that she had made. It was interesting that she would not let anyone except me enter her hospital room until she had put on her wig (radiotherapy having made her lose all her hair).

The dying patient

A busy hospital ward is not the best setting in which to die. Dying patients need relief from distressing symptoms, pain and the fear of pain. They need an environment of caring where their needs can be met without their feeling a burden and where their individuality and integrity as a person can be maintained. Patients need the time and opportunity to voice their fears, to come to terms with themselves and their illness, and to draw closer to their families. Admission to a hospice or returning home is not always possible, but successful management of pain in combination with psychological support for patients and their families can be achieved even on a busy hospital ward.

Confidentiality

Regarding confidentiality, a patient has to understand that one is working as part of a team and that information that is relevant will have to be disclosed to one or more other team members. Consent for this must be obtained from the patient. Usually this does not present a problem, although many patients will agree only if they are assured that sensitive material (for example, that they have served a prison term) will not be written up in the notes. Another instance is when patients try to insist that information they disclose will not be revealed to their GP because they have been critical of their GP's handling of their case, or when they have revealed a difficulty in their relationship with a spouse or a close relative who shares the same GP as they fear that the information will inadvertently become known to the other party.

The issue of confidentiality is also important in regard to research. Many patients understand the need for research to be carried out and wish to help. This desire to co-operate with research projects is often very strong in elderly patients and those who are terminally ill. My own research has shown that pain patients differ both from normal controls and from psychiatric patients. For another study I devised a euphoria scale to measure the effects of a new morphine substitute. I have also been involved when the hospital's 'Do not resuscitate' policy was being amended, and with a study to ascertain the efficacy of ECT in the treatment of patients with chronic thalamic pain.

Satisfaction

Research has shown that the degree to which a patient complies with advice given during a consultation with the doctor is linked to the patient's level of satisfaction with the consultation. A doctor with a friendly, understanding manner who provides information and meets the expectations of the patient is the ideal. This also applies to other healthcare professionals working with patients. Some time ago I devised simple questionnaires to assess the patient's satisfaction with the consultation with the psychologist and another to assess the doctor's satisfaction with the psychologist's findings. These are in Appendix 8.1 and Appendix 8.2 respectively. Appendix 8.3 contains the form I complete regarding, amongst other things, my rating of the suitability of the referral. One or all three forms can be used as a basis for discussion of individual patients with the referrer. It can be a useful way of training new staff in assessing which patients might benefit most from a psychological intervention.

Pitfalls

In a busy setting such as a teaching hospital there are tremendous time pressures, both in terms of time spent with patients and time initially assessing which patients could benefit from a psychological approach. As a result of this many patients who could benefit are missed altogether. Also, there is a lack of time in which to discuss patients with other members of the team, some of whom will have to leave the clinic hastily to scrub up for the operating theatre and take on their other clinical roles.

A major problem is ensuring an adequate level of supervision, as there are few supervisors qualified in this field. Peer group supervision by members of one's own discipline is less useful with intractable pain patients than with other patient groups as the patient population differs from a psychiatric population with which the peer group would be familiar.

Trying to change an ethos in which it is ensured that patients remain passive recipients of the treatment, forcing the patients to regress takes time. Patients who fail to conform to what is expected of them as medical patients on a hospital ward can also create problems. This tends to happen late on a Friday afternoon when the ward staff fear that they will be left with a difficult patient complaining of pain over the weekend, without recourse to the pain team. The staff on the medical wards do have to deal with demanding patients and they need and value psychological support and training.

It is important that the psychologist or counsellor is seen by the patient to be a member of the pain team, therefore attendance at the pain relief unit sessions in the outpatients department is essential. Arranging to see the patient outside of the pain team setting presents problems. Patients who require more time allotted than it is possible to give in a busy outpatient pain clinic have to be very gently persuaded to attend appointments in my office in the Department of Psychological Medicine.

Another problem is merely having the 'heart-sink' patients referred. Many patients expect a miracle cure once they have been referred to the pain team. Increasingly patients are becoming more litigious; also advertisements on television are encouraging patients to seek compensation on a 'no win, no fee' basis. Patients who are pursuing a compensation claim are likely to be much more difficult to engage in a treatment programme as an improvement might lead to financial loss.

Patients can find it frustrating if they never see the same doctor twice. It is far better that one member of the multidisciplinary team gets to know the patient. This saves time as the patient does not have to repeat his/her history at each visit and is more satisfying for the health professional. Good liaison between the team members, the family and any outside agency involved with the patient is essential. There is a need to be aware of what resources are available elsewhere, for example there may be a counsellor in the patient's GP surgery who could take over the patient's care. It is important to clarify for patients that your concern is with their perception of pain, rather than with pain. It is vital not to break down the patient's defences until new ones are established.

The referrers to the pain team vary from those who view the team as making a very positive contribution to the management of patients to those who view it as 'a nice dumping ground for desperate patients', to quote the director of the pain team. The 'got to learn to live with it' message frequently given by physicians and surgeons does not instil hope in the patient. Getting them to voice their fears is very important; some of the fears may be irrational or unlikely to materialise. Improving their self-esteem and setting realistic goals should be major aims in any counselling of intractable pain patients. It is unfortunate that the successful treatment of a chronic pain patient is an invisible economy from the hospital's point of view as the treated patient ceases to be part of the published statistics.

The future

The most important factor in the management of pain and in preventing it from becoming intractable pain is early intervention. More resources are needed to ensure that waiting lists for pain clinics are substantially reduced. The earlier a patient can be seen the more damage limitation can be achieved. Increasing the resources would prove extremely cost-effective. An ideal would be for every new patient to be assessed when referral is made to a pain relief unit. The aim could then be to assess those patients most likely to benefit from counselling. It would be better still to have counsellors or psychologists involved at an earlier stage in the patient's path towards becoming a chronic pain patient, for example through attendance at general medical or surgical outpatient clinics.

Most treatments of a physical nature are invasive, many are painful and some have unpleasant side-effects. Pain that has become chronic has a devastating effect not only on the patients, but also on their families and/or carers. Working as a psychologist or as a counsellor with intractable pain patients within a multidisciplinary team is both varied and satisfying, 'But if there is any single quality that working with pain patients calls for above all else it must be empathy – one needs to be able to imagine what chronic suffering is like' (Humphrey 1989).

Appendix 8.1

PAIN CLINIC/PSYCHOLOGY AUDIT: PATIENT QUESTIONNAIRE

(For questions 1 to 4 please circle either YES or NO)

1 Were you surprised at being referred to a
   psychologist?   YES   NO

2 Was the psychologist's intervention what you
   expected it to be?   YES   NO

3 Were you able to discuss things with the
   psychologist that you had not discussed with the
   doctor?   YES   NO

4 Do you feel more positively about your problem?   YES   NO

5 To what extent were you able to benefit from this
   service?
   (Please tick as appropriate)

   Being able to talk about things?   ☐

   Being listened to?   ☐

   Feel that you understand the problem better?   ☐

   Have been advised what to do?   ☐

6 How useful was the psychologist's intervention for
   you?
   (Please tick one of the boxes)   Very useful   ☐
                                             Useful   ☐
                                             Not useful   ☐
Comments:

....

....

....

Thank you for taking the time to complete this questionnaire

Appendix 8.2

PAIN CLINIC/PSYCHOLOGY AUDIT
[To be completed post-assessment by the referrer]

Patient's name: ....

Hospital no.: ....

Referred by: ....

POST-REFERRAL QUESTIONNAIRE

1 Was the psychologist's intervention what you
   expected it to be?   YES   NO

2 Did the psychologist find out additional information
   that could be pertinent to the patient's pain problem?   YES   NO

3 How satisfied are you with the amount of help the
   psychologist gave this patient?

Not at all satisfied	Not very satisfied	Neither satisfied nor dissatisfied	Satisfied	Very satisfied
1	2	3	4	5

4 What made you decide to refer this patient to the psychologist?

....

....

....

....

Thank you for taking the time to complete this questionnaire

Appendix 8.3

PAIN CLINIC/PSYCHOLOGY AUDIT
[To be completed by the psychologist]

Patient's name: . . . .

Hospital no.: . . . .

Referred by: . . . .

Sex (0 = Male; 1 = Female)   ☐

Age ☐☐

Psychiatric factors
 1 Depression   ☐
 2 Anxiety   ☐
 3 Psychosis   ☐
 4 Para-suicide/suicidal ideation   ☐
 5 Alcohol abuse   ☐
 6 Drug abuse   ☐
 7 Dementia   ☐
 8 Social problems   ☐
 9 Personality disorder   ☐
10 Neurosis   ☐
11 Mental handicap   ☐
12 Adjustment reaction   ☐
13 No psychiatric disorder   ☐

Psycho-social assessment
 1 Adjustment problems in physical illness   ☐
 2 Marital/partner difficulties   ☐
 3 Bereavement or other loss   ☐
 4 Work problems   ☐
 5 Social isolation   ☐
 6 Sexual problems   ☐
 7 Housing difficulties   ☐
 8 Financial problems   ☐
 9 Problems in significant others   ☐
10 Compensation   ☐

Psychiatric history
Currently receiving psychiatric treatment?
(0 = No, 1 = Yes, 9 = N/K)   ☐

Previous psychiatric history?
(0 = No, 1 = Yes, 9 = N/K)   ☐

Psychologist's findings:
1   Psychological assessment   ☐
2   Complex social problems   ☐
3   Relationship problems   ☐
4   Cognitive therapy?   ☐
5   ? Undisclosed problems   ☐

Appropriate referral?   Yes • ☐   No • ☐

HAD scores Anxiety   ☐☐
Depression   ☐☐

Disposal
1   Further ward consultations   ☐
2   For psychology O/P follow-up pain clinic   ☐
3   For psychology O/P follow-up K.C.H.   ☐
4   "   "   "   " catchment area   ☐
5   Referral to pain clinic psychiatrist   ☐
6   Referral to psychological medicine psychiatrist   ☐
7   Referral to catchment area psychiatrist   ☐
8   Referral to social worker   ☐
9   Discharged to care of GP   ☐

Formulation:

....
....
....
....

References

Breakwell, C. (1987) Mapping counselling in non-primary care sector of the NHS, report for the British Association for Counselling, Rugby: BAC.

Clarkson, P. (ed.) (1998) *Counselling Psychology: Integrating Theory, Research and Supervised Practice*, London: Routledge.

Humphrey, M. (1989) *Back Pain*, London: Routledge.

Latham, J. (1991) *Pain Control*, 2nd edn, London: Austen Cornish.

Lindsay, S.J.E. and Powell, G.E. (eds) (1997) *The Handbook of Clinical Adult Psychology*, 2nd edn, London: Routledge.

Melzack, R. and Wall, P.D. (1982) *The Challenge of Pain*, Harmondsworth, UK: Penguin.

Palmer, S. and McMahon, G. (eds) (1997) *Handbook of Counselling*, 2nd edn, London: Routledge.

Pitts, M. and Phillips, K. (eds) (1998) *The Psychology of Health: An Introduction*, 2nd edn, London: Routledge.

Chapter 9

Counselling in the hospice movement

Frances Birch

Introduction

Unlike some contexts where the need for psychological intervention is overlooked if not resisted, in the field of palliative care there is widespread acceptance of the need for psychological support for the dying and for those close to them. According to the World Health Organisation, palliative care is the active total care of patients whose disease is not responsive to curative treatment: control of pain, of other symptoms, and of psychological, social and spiritual problems is paramount (1990: 11). The National Council for Hospice and Specialist Palliative Care Services (1995) describes specialist palliative care services as integrating the physical, psychological, social and spiritual aspects of care, enabling dying patients to live with dignity and offering support to them and to their families and carers during the patient's illness and their bereavement.

However, in a survey of nearly 700 service providers, some 250 refer to having a bereavement service, only six specifically mention counsellors as team members, and most of those are reported as being employed in a dual role (Jackson and Eve 1997). Both the external factors involved in provision of counselling for the dying and the unconscious psychological mechanisms which operate when the inevitability of death must be faced are considered here in an attempt to explain the discrepancy between aims and achievement of psychological support for the dying.

In the United Kingdom, palliative care is provided for people suffering from cancer, and there are some specialist units treating children, or adults with AIDS or neurological disorders. Some 55 per cent of all cancer deaths occur in hospitals and 13 per cent in independent hospices (NCHSPCS 1995: 13) with funding from the National Health Service, from charitable grants and from public donations. As a research-based approach with analysis of outcomes and studies of patient and family attitudes is used increasingly in palliative care, funding for counselling may be difficult to justify as it is hard to provide purchasers with evidence of cost-effectiveness in a short-lived client group where outcomes are difficult to measure. This may in part account for the fact that bereavement counselling is more widely available than is counselling for the dying.

Developments in palliative care

Attitudes towards care of the dying reflect the beliefs and customs of each society. In our culture, which greatly values youth and fitness, death is most frequently encountered as entertainment or as art or in media reports where fact can so easily be confused with fiction, and where appropriate emotion may not be aroused. These days, many adults have never even seen a dead body and are afraid of having to do so, and everyone is protected from witnessing the reality of death as this society has relegated it to hospitals and hospices. Ariès (1987) describes how attitudes towards death have evolved in the West from accounts in the Middle Ages of the individual's awareness of imminent death, through a process of greater involvement of the family of the dying person, to the medicalisation of dying in the nineteenth century. Today, medical interventions employed in the hope of postponing death at times only obscure its imminent reality, making it difficult to address the patient's well-founded fears. While hospice care has usefully been extended from its primary focus on care of the dying to include respite care and day-centre facilities, this has had the disadvantage of making it easier for both staff and patients to avoid confronting mortality. Hospice expertise in symptom control is increasingly being used as a back-up for active radiotherapy and chemo-therapy for cancer patients. As the roles of hospice and acute oncology unit become blurred, hospice staff can find it difficult to acknowledge a patient's fears or to talk about death when this seems to question the oncologist's optimism.

There is a danger of losing our innate awareness of death and how to deal with it, as society cares for its dying members in institutions, especially in hospitals where dying is seen not as a part of life but as a technological failure. Hospices, where all family members can be welcomed, are often set in gardens which may provide an unconscious reminder of the natural cycle of growth, flowering, fading and death, and patients who choose to die at home, often supported by community and home care teams, may be responding to an inner awareness of their place in the cycle of generations.

Psychological aspects of death and dying

In psychodynamic terms, the existence of the hospice movement can be seen as an attempt by society to defend against direct confrontation with the intolerable feelings which death can arouse in us all. Those who work in a palliative care setting or who are responsible for its organisation need to be aware of the anxiety generated in patients and their families, in other members of the multidisciplinary team and in themselves by the proximity of death. As Menzies-Lyth pointed out, the need of the members of an organisation to use it in the struggle against anxiety leads to the development of socially structured defence mechanisms, which appear as elements in the organisation's structure, culture and mode of functioning, and an important aspect of such socially structured defence mechanisms is an attempt by individuals to externalise and give substance in objective reality to their characteristic defence mechanisms (1992: 50).

Studying interactions in work groups, Bion (1993) recognised that anxiety and other emotions can deflect the group from its primary task. There is a risk that the palliative care team, unconsciously defending against the anxiety of its members in the face of death, can be deflected from its primary task of controlling symptoms and providing support for the dying and those close to them, into activity in which the doctor, seen as the omnipotent leader of the group, feels compelled to persist in a futile medical struggle underpinned by the technological imperative, against the common enemy, death. Much is being done in hospices where the use of counselling skills is widespread to address psychological distress, but there remain depths of psychoanalytic insight to be drawn upon to increase our understanding of the plight of the dying and the bereaved, so that the care they receive may be improved. Whilst cognitive behavioural therapy with patients suffering from incurable illness has been shown to provide coping strategies and to reduce anxiety and feelings of helplessness (Greer and Moorey 1997), it may at the same time encourage denial of what is often the main source of distress, the inevitability of death. The medical model fights death by attempting to exclude it, while the analytical model considers dealing with death to be an essential part of all psychotherapeutic work.

Jung (1943) observed that life is like the course of the sun: indeed, much that occurs in early infancy appears to be mirrored in the dying process as the patient becomes increasingly dependent on carers. As the distress which threatens to overwhelm an infant needs to be held by an empathic mother, so the dying need acknowledgement of their distress in an environment in which it can be contained. Bion (1993) pointed out that a mother's failure to accept her infant's projection that it feels that it is dying results in re-introjection not 'of a fear of dying made tolerable, but a nameless dread'. At the beginning of life, we may experience terrifying emotions of isolation, separation, dependency, lack of control and so on which remain with us, more daunting if unheld, more destructive if unconscious, often to be confronted again when facing the imminent reality of death. To be able to work closely with dying patients in whom emotional distress threatens to become overwhelming or whose physical symptoms appear to have a psychological basis, members of the hospice team must be aware of their own vulnerability. The difficulty for palliative care purchaser/providers, and at times also for hospice team members, to recognise and face such fears would seem to underlie the lack of organisation of effective psychodynamic work with the dying.

Splitting and denial, typical paranoid-schizoid defences, pervade almost every aspect of provision of care for the dying, and any counselling which attempts to deal with these defences is likely to be seen as threatening. Society, seeking to contain its anxiety, consigns the dying to an institution, and within the hospice the multidisciplinary professional team may split off and project its members' fears and anxieties onto the dying patient and his or her family. The team's defence of denial and belief in its own magical immortality is severely threatened by terminal illness in patients younger than the staff or if a staff member or close relative is diagnosed as having an incurable illness. Coping strategies appear to fail temporarily and anxieties are openly discussed until defensive denial can be resumed.

In setting up a counselling service it is important to remember that the psychological tasks of the dying, which are considered in detail here, differ from those of the bereaved. For the latter, the work involves dealing with feelings of loss, anger, pain and rejection, with the possibility of a return to normality when the work is completed. The dying, on the other hand, must also face loss of control, loss of all known boundaries, and the dissolution of conscious existence, sinking, as we describe it, into unconsciousness. It is indeed a nameless dread: it is not surprising that powerful defences are employed by the individual, by the institution and by society to avoid facing this reality, and these defenses present the main obstacle to the provision of psychological support for the dying.

The structure of the hospice team

Members of the hospice multidisciplinary team meet each patient as someone requiring professional expertise and practical knowledge, and as a fellow human being needing emotional support. For the whole team, the skill of palliative care rests in the ability to work in a constantly changing area of tension as each team member attempts to hold both poles of this inner split. While the patient's practical needs must be attended to, the widespread availability of counselling skills, which many members of the team will have acquired by undertaking a counselling training or counselling skills course as part of their own professional development, should ensure that the emotional is not neglected, despite the powerful unconscious pull towards an exclusively medical view of the patient's predicament.

> An elderly man was relieved to be told that there comes a time when blood transfusions are no longer helpful. He had apologised, as if in some way to blame, for feeling no better despite treatment for his low haemoglobin level. He said what he really wanted was to be at home with his family.

Remarkably, patients often express gratitude for being told that they are dying, as this confirms what they know intuitively as an inner reality, and truth brings a freedom which pretence denies. Moreover, what one feels about death as a carer may be very different from what someone is feeling, even if the most distressing symptoms have been controlled, if still struggling with increasing weakness, loss of independence and the inability to enjoy many of the pleasures of human relationship. Sadness is appropriate in the dying, and this and even a longing for death are more likely to be eased by someone who can listen and face the distress than by the prescription of antidepressants.

To be able to talk about dying allows patient and family to share their grief. Feelings can be expressed freely, fears explored and the patient's autonomy restored as much as possible, allowing him or her to make decisions about what care would be appropriate in the circumstances. It is important that members of the multidisciplinary team are able to support a dying person unaffected by their own fears of death; and all team members need some counselling skills as each patient will choose someone with whom he or she feels at ease to speak about the greatest fears. The fact that, quite apart from a counselling relationship, a patient may confide in any member of the team must be respected, so that an opportunity to explore anxieties is not interrupted. Such exchanges occur unpredictably: patients need time to feel sufficiently at ease to discuss their fears. Not infrequently in the defensive cheerfulness of the hospice atmosphere, an important exchange will be interrupted and the moment lost, leaving patients to suppose that fears cannot be heard and that distress must be dealt with alone. There are other pitfalls in this frightening territory where it is not always clear what question is being asked.

A woman paralysed by spinal secondaries from breast cancer and who knew the diagnosis asked the chaplain if he could confirm that she had cancer, and later the same day asked the doctor if he believed in heaven. She appeared not to be seeking information but to be exploring the possibility of hope in the face of uncertainty.

Boundary issues in hospice counselling

It is generally accepted that secure boundaries are essential to provide containment for the powerful affects experienced in psychodynamic therapy. What is remarkable, given that those who are dying face the loss of all known boundaries, is the fact that the need for a containing therapeutic framework is often neglected in counselling in the hospice setting. In setting up a contract with a client, the hospice counsellor should be mindful of this and seek to enlist the understanding of his or her hospice colleagues to ensure that boundaries are maintained despite powerful unconscious pressure to ignore their importance.

As the patient's disease progresses some flexibility may be required, but the need for this can be minimised, and the therapeutic framework will be strengthened with co-operation of all the members of the team. Counselling sessions can usually be scheduled for times when input from other team members, such as drug rounds or nursing care, is unlikely to be needed. With the dying, as with other clients, the counselling relationship is entered into only by mutual and explicit agreement which involves a clear explanation of the terms of the contract. Other hospice team members need to know that this relationship has been embarked upon, as their involvement will be required to ensure that secure boundaries are maintained.

The following boundaries are important in work with the dying:

- time: – appointment time and frequency of sessions
          – duration of sessions,
          – duration of counselling;
- ending;

- place;
- nature of the counselling relationship;
- confidentiality;
- knowledge.

In the discussion which follows, the interaction between these boundaries will be explored. '

Time and the ending

The different aspects of time are particularly relevant in work with the dying and can be used creatively by a counsellor who is aware of their significance. Setting up a time-limited contract immediately touches on issues of ending and separation which can usefully be discussed, as the patient's greatest anxieties are often in this area. When the number of sessions is limited by the funding allocation for counselling in the institution, the stage is set for seeing management in a malign omnipotent role like death itself, and counsellors should be alert to the feelings this may arouse in themselves, in the client or in other members of the team. Of course, in the hospice context, 'open-ended' work is also time-limited when the ending, the crossing of the ultimate boundary between life and death, is beyond the control of both patient and counsellor. Recognition of this fact allows exploration of feelings about other areas of life where death does not allow time to complete all that was hoped for.

There may be an internal pressure on the counsellor to limit work in an attempt to avoid such an ending, as well as external financial pressure from a utilitarian management looking for statistics to indicate brief work with as many clients as possible. Counsellors need to be aware of their own stance so that limited contracts are not used to avoid their feelings of helplessness and distress because of separation, loss and unfinished work: regular supervision can provide an important safeguard. Time-limited contracts may be undertaken with the intention of addressing issues of time within the work; or an open-ended contract can be set up, acknowledging that death may preclude completion of at least some aspects of the psychological work. From the start it is then possible to link the limits of therapeutic time with the limited life-span, while working with the uncertainty that each session could be the last.

Time and place

Time is often distorted in the dying process and, as in childhood, there may be little awareness of passing time, chronological time or the difference between night and day. The boundary of the session, at a fixed time and for a fixed duration, may allow dying patients to retain some contact with the reality of time, alleviating their fears as they deal with the transition from existential time to the timelessness of the unconscious. Hallucinations and distortions in space as well as time can occur in the dying process and may be experienced as the threat of madness. A counsellor who can face and acknowledge such confusion will do much to reduce the patient's fears.

Counsellors who reduce the duration of sessions from the standard fifty minutes may be motivated by their own unconscious fear of facing death rather than by a need to accommodate the specific requirements of the seriously ill. As the disease progresses, the patient will become weaker and may become drowsy, confused and lose consciousness. However, there is no obligation on the dying (or on any other client for that matter) to speak or even to stay awake throughout the session, and shortening the session could put pressure on the client to attempt to remain alert while the counsellor is present. Sleep may be equated with death, and insomnia in the dying is often caused by fear of death during sleep. It is more helpful therefore to explore the dying patient's feelings about falling asleep, to allow recognition that the counsellor is not perturbed by the patient's drifting into unconsciousness but will stay with the patient until the end of the session if this should happen. An important part of psychodynamic counselling is a willingness to remain with the client in a fearful, unknowing place, and this is an essential feature of work with the dying.

At the initial meeting it is reasonable to consider the possibility of having to alter the venue for sessions from the usual consulting room to an in-patient room in the hospice, and to discuss whether other arrangements could be made if the client is at home or is admitted to hospital and unable to travel to the hospice. It is preferable to discuss these eventualities at the initial meeting rather than having to renegotiate contracts later as this may leave the client with unnecessary anxiety. Of all the boundaries, place is the one where flexibility is most likely to be needed in work with the dying.

Confidentiality

Normally, the non-duality of the counselling relationship is taken for granted, that is, the client and counsellor have a clear understanding that they meet only for the purpose of counselling and that what happens at that meeting remains strictly confidential. Unlike the United States, where Medicare reimbursement regulations require that a counsellor is included in every hospice team, the lack of specialist counsellors in palliative care in the UK results in a blurring of roles and doubts about the necessity for confidentiality in the relationship.

Working Party Clinical Guidelines (NCHSPCS 1995) suggest that community nursing teams may advise on treatment, counsel patients, and support staff and families, and that social workers will offer help with psychological, domestic, financial and legal problems. Staffing arrangements in many hospices rely on nurses and social workers in dual roles to provide counselling as necessary to patients and relatives, and sometimes to provide staff support as well. This may have financial advantages, but it has great psychological drawbacks and important implications for the boundaries of confidentiality which the professionals involved may find particularly stressful. It is a challenge to remain in touch with the patient's fears and hopelessness as a counsellor when one has the option of adopting the role of helpful social worker or caring nurse or powerful doctor who will change the medication. Such dual roles can activate an inner split in the counsellor and result in ethical dilemmas over confidentiality issues, which are even greater if the counsellor is working both with the patient and with members of his or her family.

Although not universally accepted, the professional standards expected of counsellors in the UK require that confidentiality be maintained even after the patient's death. Without the patient's consent, confidentiality may be broken only in exceptional circumstances to prevent harm to the client or to others.

> An elderly man appeared withdrawn, refusing analgesia and declining nursing care. In a counselling session, he spoke about how, as a 19-year-old, he had left an injured comrade on the battlefield, promising to return with a stretcher; but the officer in command refused to let him go as it was too risky. At last, able to express his guilt and grief, he understood why it was so hard to accept help himself as he was dying. There was no need for the counsellor to explain this to other members of the team as the man could then allow himself to be cared for.

Though information may be shared with the client's consent, to do so may weaken the therapeutic alliance and risk jeopardising the counselling work, which requires secure boundaries if it is to provide adequate containment for the powerful emotions which clients who are dying must face. It is, of course, within the counsellor's remit to question why clients cannot themselves convey information if doing so might be helpful. This may prevent a damaging conspiracy of silence in which patients find themselves unable to share their fears with relatives whose enforced cheerfulness is a reciprocal attempt to protect them.

Duality of professional roles and the suggestion that confidences can be shared with the bereaved indicate the counsellor's need to feel omnipotent, as if he or she can ensure that everything will be all right in the end. The importance of these issues may be underestimated by members of the management team, themselves having difficulty in facing the reality of death and concerned at the cost implications if specialist counsellors are included in the hospice team. These difficulties link with the final boundary, that of truth and the limits of knowledge, which is challenged in many areas of palliative care.

Knowledge, truth and the dying

The essence of counselling the dying is to be in a fearful unknowing place with the client, facing his or her imminent death in the knowledge of one's own inevitable death. This is the truth of the situation. From the medical perspective of the hospice team, fear can be allayed to some extent by knowledge, which allows the possibility of a degree of control. Working Party Guidelines suggest that the patient's needs are similar: to know the diagnosis and its implications, treatment options and their likely outcome, and what symptoms may be expected and what can be done about them; as well as having the right to deny the illness (NCHSPCS 1995). Medical knowledge may help the patient and is an important aspect of respect for autonomy, so that informed decisions can be made about what treatment is to be undertaken. However, the doctor's need to be in control in a frightening situation may make it hard for him or her to admit the limits of his or her knowledge, whilst the patient's need for information may be to obscure the unbearable truth of impending death.

> A nurse consulted her general practitioner for two years about abdominal pain, which he attributed to her age, before metastatic cancer was diagnosed by a locum. She subsequently attended a hospice day-centre and at her weekly visits asked the doctor for details about the precise location of secondaries and possible changes in serum electrolytes as if her life depended on this knowledge. Had counselling been available, she might more usefully have explored her fears about dying and her anger with the doctor and with her elderly mother for whom she was still caring.

Requests for a prognosis are often answered by an educated guess based on the doctor's wish for omniscience, but are usually better explored in terms of an acknowledgement that there is much which cannot be known precisely and how frightening this can be. In areas like this, there is the potential for conflict between a counsellor working with uncertainty and a medical team seeking to reduce anxiety with science. If such conflicts develop, patients' anxiety will increase and they may lose touch with their innate knowledge of their predicament which, as Ariès (1987) points out, was not peculiar to medieval man. Such knowledge can empower patients whose physical symptoms have been controlled to take some control of their dying; to understand what is happening within themselves rather than becoming unnecessarily dependent on an institution.

> A 22-year-old man was dying from widespread cancer. In hospital, dying was not mentioned and he discharged himself to spend time at home with his wife and infant son. As he observed dryly to the home-care sister dressing his laparotomy wound: 'It had to be pretty serious for them to have done all this to me.' Instinctively, he knew that he was facing death, and he had made his own decision about how he would deal with it.

Alone, this young man had reached the point where he could relinquish his hopes for the future, find meaning in the past, and be content in the present. Some dying patients, however, do need the input of a counsellor in order to face the anger, fear and psychological pain which must be dealt with before it is possible to accept the inevitability of death, so that the time remaining can be lived as fully as possible without clinging to false hopes.

A case study

Mrs A had been attending the hospice day-centre for some weeks, and staff were concerned because, although she was uncomplaining, she seemed withdrawn, anxious and in pain. An appointment with the day-centre doctor was arranged and she accepted mild analgesics, but it was still hard to make any real contact with her, so at the team meeting a referral was made to the hospice counsellor.

In the first session, Mrs A spoke in a detached way about her illness, a sad end to a sad life. She had declined home-care team involvement and planned to be admitted to the hospice when she could no longer cope at home. She agreed to an open-ended counselling contract though she left the counsellor with the sense that she did not expect this to be helpful, but did not want to offend the counsellor by refusing. It was planned that they would meet each week at the same time and place, but that if admitted later to the ward she could be seen there. As Mrs A talked about herself, an increasingly bleak picture of her life emerged. She had had to give up her work with a youth project when she became ill, but despite weakness and pain, she managed to keep her house neat and clean as she had always done. She struggled with shopping and cooked for her husband, eating little herself on account of her increasing nausea. She was adamant that her husband was too busy to help with the chores and, months ago, she had moved into the spare bedroom lest her restless nights should deprive him of the sleep he needed to continue with his professional work.

The counsellor grappled with her feelings of hopelessness as time seemed to be running out. In supervision she questioned the obligations of her role as counsellor – should she or another team member talk to Mr A? In team meetings, other members of the team expressed their anger with Mr A and their critical comments added to the counsellor's sense of her own powerlessness. Her repeated suggestions that more help might be available only met with Mrs A's insistence that she could cope. It seemed that all the counsellor could do was to witness the distress and accept that there might be no resolution.

The following week, the hospice transport was late. The counsellor felt a sense of relief – only ten minutes left of what usually felt like an unbearably long session! Then guilt took over; Mrs A must be getting something from the sessions, so should she perhaps make up the lost time? She resolved to hold the boundary, and a rather subdued Mrs A said with resignation and barely concealed annoyance that it was fine: she'd had a better week; there wasn't much to say anyway. The glimmerings of anger startled the counsellor from her depressed feelings: 'But maybe it does feel a bit like being sent to boarding school when you were seven and your parents had just separated: when you thought there was someone you could rely on, and suddenly there was no-one around and you had to deal with everything yourself.' Mrs A's eyes filled with tears and she sobbed silently. The counsellor suggested that the illness might repeat that situation: something very frightening which had to be faced alone. Mrs A nodded, and when the session was due to end she said: 'I'd better go now, or they will be wondering in the day-centre where I am – but I *will* see you next week.'

At the next session, Mrs A announced that her husband had brought her today: 'I was a bit upset after last week, so he said he'd take the morning off.' At last, she had been able to tell him how she felt and to accept his support. A month later, she asked if the home-care team would visit as she had decided that she wanted to die at home, and Mr A had arranged to have time off from work when she needed full-time care. He was already doing some of the housework, and Mrs A spoke in the sessions about her surprise that she did not have to deal with everything alone and that she could still be valued though by now she was extremely weak physically. Mrs A said she knew it would be hard to say goodbye, but she suggested that she would no longer need the sessions when she stopped attending the day-centre: 'I know now that I shall be well looked after.'

Role of the counsellor in the palliative care team

There are two closely linked factors which limit the availability of counselling expertise to patients suffering from terminal illness: the lack of recognition of what counselling has to offer to this client group and the lack of funding to provide it. At present, the counsellor in palliative care may need to face the hostility of other members of the multidisciplinary or management team who deal with their fear of death by continuing to deny it as they act out a manic defence. The benefits of counselling are more easily felt than measured and hard to convey to purchaser/providers, who see the activity of the hospice team in terms of bed-occupancy and throughput.

It is up to the counsellor to acknowledge and to keep the team mindful of the stress which every death causes. When pressure on beds demands their reuse soon after someone has died, the counsellor can remind the team that psychological space is still needed for that person even if physical space is no longer available. At the multidisciplinary team meeting, which often has a medical emphasis, the counsellor may be able to ensure that the team does not lose its psychological awareness, and without having to share confidential information with the team, can draw attention to the presence of emotional distress which may be contributing to the patient's symptoms.

Launer's (1994) account of psychotherapeutic work in a general practice surgery indicates that the difficulties encountered in a multidisciplinary team involving medical care can be overcome with co-operation between team members and an openness to critical analysis of the work carried out, a useful model of what could be achieved in a hospice setting. Hospice staff groups tend to increase the split in the team as only the psychologically minded attend, but the counsellor's input in team meetings and discussions of patient care can maintain psychological awareness while promoting respect for different approaches resulting from the expertise of individual team members. The counsellor plays a central role in holding together both inner and outer splits while aiming to achieve a wholeness which is also the goal of work with individual clients.

The primary aim of hospice counselling must be to contain the anxiety which is inevitable in the face of death, to ensure that the 'fear of dying [is] made tolerable' (Bion 1993). Defences against this fear are currently so widespread that they interfere with the provision of adequate psychological care for the dying, and lack of research and outcome studies allows providers to ignore the importance of counselling in the hospice setting.

Inherent in all of us is the tension between a desire for immortality and the knowledge of our mortality. The hospice counsellor must work in an environment where this tension is exacerbated, first, by the exigencies of the technological imperative, and second, by the tendency for the direct relationship between counsellor and client to be blurred by the competing needs of relatives and staff, and by the financial limits set by society. The progress that has been made in palliative care in the treatment of physical symptoms is widely acknowledged, but avoidable psychological suffering of the dying will be mitigated only when those who recognise the potential of hospice counselling make themselves heard.

References

Ariès, P. (1987) *The Hour of Our Death*, Harmondsworth, UK: Penguin.

Bion, W.R. (1993) *A Theory of Thinking in Second Thoughts*, London: Karnac.

Greer, S. and Moorey, S. (1997) 'Adjuvant Psychological Therapy for Cancer Patients', *Palliative Medicine* **11**: 240–4.

Jackson, A. and Eve, A. (eds) (1997) *Directory of Hospice and Palliative Care Services in the United Kingdom and Republic of Ireland*, London: Hospice Information Service, St Christopher's Hospice.

Jung, C.G. (1943) *Two Essays on Analytical Psychology*, reprinted in *The Collected Works of C.G. Jung*, eds. H. Read, M. Fordham and G. Adler, vol. 7, New York: Pantheon, 1955.

Launer, J. (1994) 'Psychotherapy in the General Practice Surgery: Working With and Without a Secure Therapeutic Frame', *British Journal of Psychotherapy* **11** (1): 120–6.

Menzies-Lyth, I. (1992) *Containing Anxiety in Institutions*, London: Free Association.

Working Party on Clinical Guidelines in Palliative Care (1995) *Information for Purchasers: Background to Available Specialist Palliative Care Service*, National Council for Hospice and Specialist Palliative Care Services.

World Health Organisation (1990) *Cancer Pain Relief and Palliative Care: Report of a WHO Expert Committee*, Technical Report 804, Geneva: WHO.

Index